The Economy of God:

A Practical Commentary on Ephesians

Howard A. Snyder

Urban Loft Publishers | Skyforest, CA

Write:

Urban Loft Publishers

P.O. Box 6

Skyforest, CA. 92385

www.urbanloftpublishers.com

ISBN: 978-0-9973717-4-1

Manufactured in the U.S.A

Editors: Stephen Burris & Kendi Howells Douglas

Copy Editor: Michelle Munson

Graphics: Elisabeth Clevenger & Amber McKinley

Table of Contents

Series Preface

Urban Mission in the 21st Century is a series of monographs that addresses key issues facing those involved in urban ministry whether it be in the slums, squatter communities, *favelas*, or in immigrant neighborhoods. It is our goal to bring fresh ideas, a theological basis, and best practices in urban mission as we reflect on our changing urban world. The contributors to this series bring a wide-range of ideas, experiences, education, international perspectives, and insight into the study of the growing field of urban ministry. These contributions fall into four very general areas: 1--the biblical and theological basis for urban ministry; 2--best practices currently in use and anticipated in the future by urban scholar/activists who are living working and studying in the context of cities; 3--personal experiences and observations based on urban ministry as it is currently being practiced; and 4--a forward view toward where we are headed in the decades ahead in the expanding and developing field of urban mission. This series is intended for educators, graduate students, theologians, pastors, and serious students of urban ministry.

More than anything, these contributions are creative attempts to help Christians strategically and creatively think about how we can better reach our world that is now more urban than rural. We do not see theology and practice as separate and distinct. Rather, we see sound practice growing out of a healthy vibrant theology that seeks to understand God's world as it truly is as we move further into the twenty-first century. Contributors interact with the best scholarly literature available at the time of writing while making application to specific contexts in which they live and work.

Each book in the series is intended to be a thought-provoking work that represents the author's experience and perspective on urban ministry in a particular context. The editors have chosen those who bring this rich diversity of perspectives to this series. It is our hope and prayer that each book in this series will challenge, enrich, provoke, and cause the reader to dig deeper into subjects that bring the reader to a deeper understanding of our urban world and the ministry the church is called to perform in that new world.

Dr. Kendi Howells Douglas and Stephen Burris,
Urban Mission in the 21st Century Series Co-Editors

Introduction

Ecclesiological laments are very common. They have been through the centuries, in fact. Repeatedly writers denounce the infidelity of the church.

This certainly has been true throughout my lifetime. For decades I have heard Christian leaders and thinkers complain that the church does not pay nearly enough attention to the question of precisely *what the church is* and how God intends it to *function* in his larger plan or economy (*oikonomia*) for the kingdom of God.

I hear this lament particularly with regard to Evangelicalism. Evangelicals are by definition activists trying to win as many people as possible to saving faith in Jesus Christ. In the process the priority of conversion evangelism—"getting people saved"— often trumps deeper questions about being saved *to what* and *for what purpose* in God's economy. In other words, this is the question of *the church*.[1]

The irony, of course, is that the New Testament is full of teaching about the church. In fact the New Testament says much more about the nature and function of the church than it does about evangelism. Nowhere is this clearer than in Paul's letter to the Ephesians.

---

[1] See John G. Stackhouse, Jr., ed., *Evangelical Ecclesiology: Reality or Illusion?* (Grand Rapids: Baker Academic, 2003), and in particular my chapter, "The Marks of Evangelical Ecclesiology," 77–103).

The book of Ephesians is crucially important. In his book *The Day the Revolution Began*, N.T. Wright comments: "I have often reflected that if the Reformers had focused on Ephesians rather than Romans or Galatians, the entire history of Western Europe would have been different." He adds, "What might happen if, instead of the ultimate vision of saved souls going to heaven, we were to start with the eschatology of Ephesians 1:10, with God's plan to sum up all things in heaven and earth in the Messiah?"[2]

Precisely. This is my aim in the present book — which means, among other things, showing clearly what *church* means.

So, what is the church? This question troubled me with increasing insistence for years. Especially when I began pastoring a church—the Redford Free Methodist Church in Detroit—in 1966.

But I was convinced of one thing. The only way to find the answer is through the study of sacred Scripture. Throughout most of 1971 and into 1972 therefore, while my family and I were living in Brazil, I conducted a continuous study of the Epistle to the Ephesians. There, I felt, I would find an authoritative answer to the question: What is the church, biblically understood?

The material offered in this book, refined over four decades of ministry and further thought, is the result. The book is largely interaction with and reflection upon the Word. It relates what are for me some highly surprising and significant insights into the biblical nature of the church and of God's kingdom plan. This study transformed my whole conception and perception of the church of Jesus Christ. It also led eventually to dealing more fully with the

---

[2] N.T. Wright, *The Day the Revolution Began* (New York: HarperCollins, 2016), 33, 49.

question of the kingdom of God and the relationship between church and kingdom. When I published *The Problem of Wineskins* in 1975, I noted that my intensive study of the book of Ephesians during 1971 had been key to the insights in that work.

Readers familiar with my book *The Community of the King* will recognize that the letter to the Ephesians was foundational for that book, as well. Some of the chapters in that book grew directly from this study. The whole of *The Community of the King* in fact reflects Paul's teachings on the church in Ephesians, though substantially enriched by the whole corpus of Scripture. In fact, my Ephesians study served as a basis for most of my books, in particular *Salvation Means Creation Healed.*[3]

The book falls naturally into six chapters, following the six chapters of Paul's letter. The concluding section summarizes the epistle's teaching on the church in God's plan.

This small book is not a full commentary on Ephesians. Such commentaries abound, and I cite some in the course of my discussion. The special focus here is God's plan (*oikonomia*) and the church within that plan. This is in fact Paul's focus. We necessarily will look also at other topics Ephesians mentions such as marriage, principalities and powers, and of course Christology. Ephesians in fact is fundamentally about Jesus Christ, Head and body. Throughout the discussion I give particular focus to matters that are, in my estimation, especially relevant to the church in our day and time.

Though not a comprehensive commentary, the book closely

---

[3] Howard A. Snyder with Joel Scandrett, *Salvation Means Creation Healed: The Ecology of Sin and Grace* (Eugene, Ore.: Cascade Books, 2011).

follows the biblical text, often verse by verse. I deal mainly with the English text. Mostly I use the NRSV, though occasionally I employ others, or (rarely) my own translation, that bring out the original meaning more clearly. I have found that in several instances the older RSV is more succinct and sometimes clearer than the NRSV, so I make use of both. (Unless otherwise indicated, all biblical quotations are from the NRSV.)

I began this study with the simple aim of understanding the church. I needed that understanding for my own ministry. But the church focus quickly expanded to a concern to understand God's overall plan—God's "economy" for the world. The very first chapter of Ephesians pushes us in that direction.

Ephesians is one of the few New Testament letters that says nothing bad about the church! We know of the problems at Corinth, in Galatia, and elsewhere. But here: Not a word of criticism or reproof!

Was Ephesus, then, a model church? Do we have here the "New Testament church" in its purest form? Is this the true model, the true early church?

Two immediate problems stop us from taking the Ephesian church as ecclesiological perfection.

First, we are not sure the letter was directed only to the Ephesian Christians. The document was likely a circular letter intended for several churches. This may explain the letter's more general focus.

Second, perhaps as a consequence, Paul does not seem to be describing a particular local church so much as giving an overall picture of God's action in forming the church. Perhaps no particular local church is specifically in view.

But there is another side to this coin. Though Ephesians may not be a portrait of a specific church the way the Corinthian letters are, Paul certainly has in mind *actual churches* he had seen and visited. In most cases, he had founded them.

So the picture of the church in Ephesians is not "dreamed up." It is not an airy ideal church never actually grounded in space and time. This is important. The picture of the church here is very much rooted in history. When Paul writes of spiritual gifts, building community, or facing spiritual powers, he is describing the day-by-day experience of actual believers he knew by name. But he is doing more: He is reflecting theologically on what this means. He is saying, in effect: *This is what God has done—as you very well know. You are part of it. Now, here is what it means.*

Ephesians does then give us a model for the church — perhaps the clearest, most profound and concise picture of the church in all Scripture. Yet this is not an idealized picture floating somewhere in space or "in the heavenlies" which never really touches down to earth to our nitty-gritty lives. Rather, here is a picture of what the church most profoundly *is*, and what it can be in actual space and time.

Furthermore, Ephesians pictures the church in interaction with culture and with "principalities and powers." In this discussion I deal with the important issues of culture, power, economics, and politics. I occasionally refer to writings in such fields as history, sociology, anthropology, and economics. In order to keep the book uncluttered, I generally do not cite the specific sources that lie behind these comments or references.

Paul's profound but realistic picture of the church is what makes Ephesians so intensely relevant—and exciting—today.

Chapter 1

God's Plan: All Space and Time

Early Christian writers spoke of "the economy of God," meaning the whole sweep of God's redemptive plan centering in Jesus Christ.[4] The term "economy" actually comes from a key New Testament word, *oikonomia,* which means an overall plan for managing a household (*oikos*). New Testament English versions variously translate the word as "stewardship," "plan," "administration," "commission" (NRSV), or even "dispensation" (King James Version).

In the Greco-Roman culture of Apostle Paul's day, *oikonomia* had a broad meaning. It could be applied to the administration or management of a city. A related word was *oikomene,* which meant the whole inhabited earth (that is, the whole human family) and is the basis for our English word "ecumenical." (The very use of the word *economy* in this context is a hint that economics in the modern financial sense also falls within the much larger economy of God, since here is the cultural context in which the whole idea of *economy* finds its roots.)

For Paul, *economy* was thus a good word for speaking of God's

---

[3] See especially G. L. Prestige, *God in Patristic Thought* (London: SPCK, 1952), 57-59, 62-63, 98-102.

overall redemptive plan.[5] This is his focus especially in the book of Ephesians. Paul puts God's plan in the largest possible context. And in this context, he speaks of what he calls "the heavenly places" or "heavenly realms."

Where are "The Heavenly Places"?

Insight into God's overall plan through the church comes early in the letter when Paul for the first time refers to "the heavenly places," in Ephesians 1:3.

1:3 — in the heavenly places.

A peculiar phrase, it occurs five times in Ephesians—but nowhere else in Paul's writings. So it's a good place to begin our investigation of God's plan.

The phrase is probably best taken just as it is—God "has blessed us in Christ with every spiritual blessing in the heavenly places." It is simply misleading to translate the phrase "blessings from heaven" or "heavenly blessings," as some commentaries suggest. In fact in the original Greek the word "places" does not occur. The word is simply "the heavenlies."

Here we first encounter one of the basic and unique characteristics of this epistle: its *cosmic aspect*. Ephesians 1 puts God's plan through Jesus Christ and through the church not just on an earthly plane, but at the center of the divine will for the entire cosmos! God has blessed us in Christ, not merely with "heavenly blessings," nor merely with the future promise of heaven, but "with

---

5 We will note later that *economy of God* and *kingdom of God* are actually closely related concepts and realities, and in some contexts can be virtually synonymous.

every spiritual blessing in the heavenly places."

In other words, we are more than just citizens of this temporal world. As spiritual beings, and in Christ, we inhabit God's cosmos, the essential nature of which is spiritual, though it also has material dimensions. We have not yet attained heaven, but we are already blessed "in the heavenly realms."

This becomes clearer as we look at the other instances of this phrase:

1:20-21 — God has raised Christ from the dead "and seated him at his right hand in the heavenly places, far above all rule and authority and power and dominion."

2:6 — God also "raised us up with him and seated us with him in the heavenly places in Christ Jesus."

3:10 — God's plan is that "through the church the wisdom of God in its rich variety might now be made known to the rulers and authorities [KJV: principalities and powers] in the heavenly places."

6:12 — Our warfare is "against the rulers [KJV: principalities], against the authorities, against the cosmic powers of this present darkness, against the spiritual forces of evil in the heavenly places."

What then does Paul mean by "the heavenly places" or "heavenly realms"? Basically, the cosmos—the totality of God's creation, which is primarily and essentially spiritual but which includes the physical, material creation. Christ sits at God's right hand "in the heavenly places," at the center of the spiritual world. There also we now share with Christ. God's plan through the church has cosmic significance—to glorify God in the earthly created order but also "in the heavenly places"—throughout the totality of the spirit world. Our warfare therefore is not limited to "flesh and blood," but also is cosmic—against Satan and all the forces of evil under his command.

We don't know precisely how Paul understood the nature of the spiritual world—whether as various levels of spiritual beings, according to current Jewish ideas, or in some other way. That is relatively unimportant. What we do know is this: Reality is not essentially physical and material, but spiritual. The created material world is fully real, but is a manifestation, or a range of dimensions, of the spiritual world. God created the material world in space and time. God is spirit, humans are essentially spirit, and the church is essentially a spiritual reality. Human physicality is part of their spirituality—the material dimension of being spiritual—not something essentially non-spiritual.

Consider a rock and the air that surrounds it. Both are physically real, though we cannot see the air's reality. Similarly, we cannot see the spiritual reality of our physical being, but it is real. In God's world, spirit and matter are not opposites. Rather, all that is material is part of all that is spiritual, because all comes from the hand of God and is sustained by him. In keeping with all of Scripture, Paul is not working with or assuming a dualism between spirit and matter. (More about this later.)

This is not philosophical idealism or speculation. The world really does exist in material form in space, time, and history. The material world is real and, as the incarnation both demonstrates and guarantees, not only real but redeemable. Yet the basic and prior and most inclusive dimension is spiritual.

So it is perfectly logical that our "warfare" or struggle is not "carnal" or "merely human" but is fundamentally spiritual; our weapons "mighty through God to the pulling down of strongholds" (2 Cor 10:4 KJV). So Christians should recognize in all things that what they are doing, and what God does, and what the church is, are essentially matters of the spirit.

Living in the heavenly realms therefore is not withdrawing from the mundane world of things and objects, sights and sounds, pollution and politics. Rather it is living *in the midst and muddle of this world*, participating in it, yet always deeply conscious of the Bigger Dimension. Perhaps it is like the returned astronaut, now conscious that the earth is part of larger space. To live in the heavenly places is, in short, to be *in* the world but not *of* it.

So "blessed be the God and Father of our Lord Jesus Christ, who has blessed us in Christ with every spiritual blessing in the heavenly places" (1:3). From this verse on in Ephesians, we are in "the heavenly places" or realms. We are seeing the church in cosmic perspective. Not merely in the future, after death, do we participate in the eternal, spiritual world; *we are now in the heavenly places.* We are citizens of God's spiritual world, yet unable easily to recognize this because of the limitations of space and time and the pollution of sin.

1:4 — "He chose us in Christ before the foundation of the world." We enter here into a second key feature of Ephesians: the will and purpose of God. God's will is mentioned about six times in Ephesians; "purpose," four times; "destined," twice; "called" or "calling," several times.[6]

Further, this divine direction and purpose is set in the context of eternity—in the cosmic perspective of which we have been speaking. We enter here the mystery of God's eternal purpose for his creation.

First of all then, we note that we live in a world governed by purpose. Many doubt this today. Many people see nothing but chaos and blind chance in the working of human affairs and in nature. But Christians share this revealed secret: God is working out his plan and purpose, his economy. The world is not left totally to chaos.

What is this divine purpose? The first three chapters of Ephesians reveal it clearly. It is, in short, that God be glorified:

> 1. through the salvation of men and women (1:1-7);
>
> 2. through the church (3:9-11);
>
> 3. through the uniting or reconciling of all things in Christ (1:10, 21-23).

But these are not really three distinct points. They are part of one whole. *God's plan is to unite all things in Christ through the church.* "To bring all things in heaven and on earth together under one head," Jesus Christ (1:10). Thus it is with God's will seen in cosmic perspective that Paul begins the doctrine of the church.

1:4 — He chose us.

The divine choice. The divine election. All biblical Christians believe in election. The crucial thing is to understand election *biblically.* God chose and destined us—those who believe—to be "holy and blameless," to be "his children through Jesus Christ." This

---

[6] The actual number of occurrences varies according to the English translation of version; however this same emphasis on God's will and purpose is equally evident in the Greek text.

is God's election, of those who believe, to be redeemed and sanctified. "For those whom he foreknew he also predestined to be conformed to the image of his Son" (Rom 8:29). Foreknowing who would accept the gospel call, God predestined that these would take on the image of his Son. Or in other words, to paraphrase slightly, "we who *first* hoped in Christ have accordingly been destined and appointed to live for the praise of his glory" (1:11-12). This election to the Christian life implies the volitional choice of each person in the sense that he or she may accept or reject. But it also implies the mystery of the operation of the Holy Spirit, by which, "for the praise of his glory" (1:12) he convicts and draws persons to himself.

1:7 — In him we have redemption through his blood, the forgiveness of our trespasses.

These first two chapters of Ephesians are important in that they clearly show *the nature of that salvation which God provides*. God's eternal plan for men and women is that they should be "his children through Jesus Christ," that they should be saved. What does this mean? As we have seen, the scope of salvation is cosmic. But at its center, salvation is *the redemption of persons*. But in what sense?

First of all, Paul says, redemption through Christ's blood is *forgiveness of sins*. This is the essential beginning of God's salvation, but not its fullness. As this passage, which runs through verse 10, shows, God's "plan (*oikonomia*) for the fullness of time to unite [RSV] all things in him, things in heaven and things on earth" (the cosmic aspect), begins with "redemption through his blood, the forgiveness of our trespasses."

Second, redemption through Christ's blood means a *new destiny*. "We who first hoped in Christ have been destined and appointed to live for the praise of his glory" (1:12 RSV). This is a new destiny, a new goal for one's life.

Third, redemption through Christ's blood is *by an act of faith*. "You . . . who have heard the word of truth, ... and have *believed* in him, were sealed with the promised Holy Spirit . . ." (1:13 RSV). "For by grace you have been saved through faith" (2:8; note also 3:17).

Fourth, this redemption is *an act of God, a gift of his grace*. "You *he* made alive, when you were dead through the trespasses and sins" (2:1 RSV). "God . . . made us alive together with Christ" (2:4-5). "It is the gift of God—not the result of works, so that no one may boast" (2:8-9).[7]

Fifth, redemption through Christ's blood is *being united in one body in Christ*. Christ "has made both groups [Jew and Gentile] into one . . . that he might . . . reconcile both groups to God in one body through the cross" (2:14-16). This is a central theme in all Paul's teaching about the church.

Finally, this redemption is *the basis for reconciliation between persons*. "For he is our peace, who has made us both one, and has broken down the dividing wall of hostility, . . . that he might create in himself one new [humanity] in place of the two, so making peace" (2:14-15 RSV).

1:9 — *He has made known to us the mystery of his will.*

God has revealed the secret—the mystery human intelligence labors unceasingly to solve—of what God is up to in the world; what

---

[7] In the Greek text the verb "made alive" occurs in 1:5, but the RSV helpfully moves it to verse 1, which clarifies Paul's long complex sentence.

he is doing; the purpose which governs all! The key secret has been revealed, and it is through Paul that God gives it the clearest expression. It is a plan "set forth in Christ for the fulness of time"; specifically, "to unite all things in him [Christ], things in heaven and things on earth" (1:10 RSV). This is God's cosmic plan, with Jesus Christ at the center.

1:10 — as a plan (oikonomia) —

This is the first occurrence of the key term *oikonomia* in Ephesians. In many translations the term is obscured by the way verses 9 and 10 are translated. The NIV for instance has "he made known to us the mystery of his will according to his good pleasure, which he purposed in Christ, to be put into effect . . . ." More literally it should read: "he made known to us the mystery of his will according to his good pleasure in Christ, *a plan* to be put into effect. . . ."

1:10 — to gather up all things in him, things in heaven and things on earth.

Once again, the cosmic aspect. God's plan is a cosmic plan. This cosmic dimension comes through over and over in Ephesians—most explicitly in 1:3-4; 1:10; 1:21-23; 2:6-7; 3:9-11; 3:15; 3:21; 4:6; 4:10; and 6:12. In discussing 3:9-10 we will necessarily give detailed attention to just what God's plan involves and what it means for the church.

This theme however is not unique to Paul. Other New Testament passages make the same point but in different ways, especially Matthew 11:27; Luke 10:22; John 3:35, 12:32. These verses can usefully be compared with Jeremiah 10:16 and, in Paul,

Romans 11:36; 1 Corinthians 15:28; and Philippians 3:21. Taken together and studied inductively, these passages all fit together in revealing God's plan of salvation through Jesus Christ by the Spirit.

It is clear from Ephesians 1:10 that God intends to "unite all things" in Christ or (more literally) "to bring all things in heaven and on earth together under one head, even Christ" (NIV). It is clear also that this divine plan, for which Jesus Christ was born, lived, suffered, died, and rose again, will not be entirely realized until this culmination—all things reconciled in Jesus Christ—actually takes place. It is clear further that this cosmic reconciling of all things in Jesus Christ will in fact take place as a real occurrence within the sphere of human history—or rather, as the climax and culmination of human history.

1:11-14 — *to the praise of his glory. . . . We who first hoped* [i.e., Jewish Christians]. . . . *You also* [i.e., Gentile converts] (RSV).

What is true of one group is true of the other. The same salvation is provided to both. And the purpose of this salvation—for Jew as well as Gentile—is that each may live "for (or to) the praise of his glory." The ultimate purpose of our salvation is that God may be glorified. In this sense the purpose of our salvation lies outside ourselves. It is not purely "subjective." Christ died that we might be saved, but God wills and provides our salvation that he may be glorified.

1:13-14 — *sealed with the promised Holy Spirit, which is the guarantee of our inheritance until we acquire possession of it* (RSV).

Ephesians is a very Christocentric book. The name "Christ,"

alone or in various combinations (Lord Jesus Christ, Christ Jesus, etc.) occurs about 50 times (depending on the English version). For this reason I say that the central focus of Ephesians is not the church, but Jesus Christ—Head and body.

Paul also repeatedly mentions the Holy Spirit—some 11 times. This is natural of course, given the Trinitarian reality of God which underlies the letter.

Christians are to be "filled with the Spirit" (5:18), and here in 1:13 Paul says each Christian has been "sealed with the promised Holy Spirit" (RSV). It is clear from the plural pronouns "our" and "we" in verse 14 that Paul is saying both Jew and Gentile converts have been thus sealed.

The meaning of this passage has been well elucidated by dozens of commentators. A few key points:

1. This sealing by the Spirit is something that occurs with every person who is converted to Christ. In other words, this "sealing" is one aspect of being converted. (Note 4:30)

2. This sealing is another way of expressing the fact that in conversion we are regenerated by the Holy Spirit; we receive a new life. The life of God, the divine nature, has entered our life and begun to reshape us. "God, who is rich in mercy, out of the great love with which he loved us even when we were dead through our trespasses, made us alive together with Christ" (2:4-5). This is the work of the Holy Spirit and the sealing of the Holy Spirit—the receiving of new life through the Spirit.

3. But in using this term, and the term "guarantee" (or "pledge" or "down payment") in verse 14, Paul here evidently is looking toward the future. We were sealed in the sense that this new life is but the beginning. What we have received now through the Holy

Spirit is merely (but essentially) the foretaste of what we will receive at the day of redemption—that is, on the day of our resurrection. What we now experience is real and divine and glorious, and yet also God's guarantee of much more to come.

This striking affirmation fits nicely into the overall theme of Ephesians—that God is bringing all things to completion in Christ.

4. This sealing does not imply that at our justification we receive all God's presence that we can and should receive in this life. Indeed, Paul explicitly affirms the opposite in 5:18 when he says "be filled with the Spirit." Every true Christian has been *sealed* with the Spirit—but Paul exhorts us also to be *filled* with the Spirit.

5. Verse 13 speaks of "the promised Holy Spirit," or "the Holy Spirit of promise" (ASV). The emphasis seems to be on the past; that in the past the Holy Spirit has been promised to those who believe. Some see a future aspect here as well—he is the Spirit of promise; that is, the Spirit who promises to realize what is not yet (for example W. Pannenberg, J. Moltmann). This is certainly valid biblically, at least indirectly, if we consider the Spirit's role throughout biblical prophecy.

The emphasis on *promise* in the revelation of God is salutary and helpful as long as it is not made to be the *one key* to the understanding of God's nature. Certainly the element of promise is present here in this passage.

Paul is saying: The Holy Spirit has been promised you (in the Old Testament, and by Christ)—and you have already received the Spirit, yet only in a partial way, as it is a foretaste of what is yet to come. The promise still holds true. And God has given us, in a real but not yet fully realized way, his presence as a guarantee of what is yet to come: the complete fulfillment of the promise.

In much the same way, Jesus' resurrection is the guarantee of the promise of our own bodily resurrection (1 Cor 15, Rom 8).

God is the God of promise. We live the present moment at the point between past promises already fulfilled and present promises to be fulfilled in the future. We see God as trustworthy because of what he has already done in fulfillment of promise and therefore have full confidence of his acts in the future. Needless to say, this certainty and confidence come through faith. This is a crucial and essential point in being the church, as Paul recognizes.

1:15 — *Your faith in the Lord Jesus and your love towards all the saints.*

The Ephesian church was characterized by faith and love. It had gotten a good reputation.

1:17 — *That the God of our Lord Jesus Christ, the Father of glory, may give you a spirit of wisdom and revelation as you come to know him* (or *in the knowledge of him,* RSV).

Here is a remarkable prayer! Paul prays that the Ephesian Christians may understand and experience what it is that God is doing.

"A spirit of wisdom and revelation." The reference here is probably to the Holy Spirit, whose function is to give wisdom to reveal, and to guide into all truth. It is difficult to conceive how the Christian could be given "a spirit of revelation" in some other sense, since in fact revelation comes of God through the Holy Spirit. Subjectively of course a person can respond to and welcome this operation of the Spirit and in that sense have "a spirit of wisdom and of revelation"—a personal harmonious response to the Spirit.

In any case, it is clear here that Paul is praying that all Christians might receive wisdom and revelation; and specifically "that the eyes of your heart may be enlightened in order *that you may know . . ."* (1:18 TNIV).

What would Paul have us know? Three things:

1. the hope to which we are called;
2. the riches of his glorious inheritance;
3. the greatness of his power (verses 18-19).

Is Paul praying here for a *deeper spiritual experience* on the part of Christians (personally, or corporately as Christ's body)? Or for *increased intellectual understanding* of the faith?

The question, of course, is not entirely valid. Spiritual growth is personal growth in Christ. Mind, body and spirit form a totality, a personal unity, so that spiritual growth is at the same time intellectual growth. Or should be. Yet on the other hand, we recognize that intellectual development without a parallel spiritual deepening is possible and in fact frequently occurs. Similarly, we certainly know that not all spiritual growth is accompanied by a corresponding greater intellectual understanding of the faith. Ideally, both should occur as part of our continuing growth.

In these verses (1:17-19), Paul is not making or assuming a distinction between mind and spirit. He is not separating spiritual growth and intellectual development. But since we do in fact often confront this problem, this separation, it helps to ask the question and point out the distinction—precisely so that we can then withdraw the distinction, reaffirming the oneness and totality of our growth in Christ.

Because this invalid distinction between spiritual and intellectual growth is so common in the church, I need to elaborate this further. Based on Paul's teaching here (in harmony with the rest of Scripture) we may affirm the following:

1. This growth in wisdom and revelation includes an increased (and increasing) intellectual understanding of the faith.

a. *This is indicated here by the use of the words "knowledge" (vs 17 KJV), and "know" (vs 18).*

We can focus on: knowledge – epignosei, or "full knowledge." This cannot refer to an experiential knowledge only which excludes the participation or enlightenment of the mind. It cannot be a knowledge based exclusively in subjective experience, without an (at least partial) intellectual understanding accompanying it and reflecting *validly* upon it.

It is instructive here to note parallel uses of this word in the New Testament—for example, Rom 1:28; 3:20; 1 Tim 2:4; 2 Tim 3:7; 2 Pt 1:2, 3; 1:28; 2:20. The term is used usually in the sense of "the full knowledge of Jesus Christ" as something to be experientially apprehended.

Romans 1:28 is particularly instructive. "And since they did not see fit to acknowledge God," or more literally, "Even as they refused to have God in their knowledge (*epignosei*)" (Karl Barth), "God gave them up to a debased mind and to things that should not be done," or, "he has given them up to their own depraved reason." This leads them to "break all rules of conduct" (NEB).

"Base mind" or "depraved reason" (*adokimon noun*) clearly refers to a morally corrupted condition of a person's rational powers. "Mind" or "reason" (*noós*) "denotes the faculty of physical and intellectual perception, and also the power to arrive at moral judgments" (Arndt and Gingrich, *Greek-English Lexicon*, 546). We are dealing here with human rational capability and human reason.

The linking together of "full knowledge" and "reason" in this passage is instructive. Paul is saying: People have chosen to exclude God from their knowledge, with the result that they have become morally corrupt in their reason, their thinking. No longer are they able to think, reason, and understand on a consistently rational basis. Their intellectual understanding has become corrupt, because God has been excluded from it.

Thus "full knowledge" in Romans 1:28 seems to include (but is not limited to) one's intellectual understanding, his or her rational capacity. If not, we would have to make a radical disjunction between the first and second part of this verse, between knowledge (as strictly experiential or existential knowledge) and reason (as strictly rational or intellectual capacity). In fact, this dichotomy is impossible. "Full knowledge" (*epignosei*) means *first of all* experiential knowledge, but *includes* rational understanding, while conversely "mind" or "reason" (*noós*) means first of all humanity's rational, intellectual capacity *but also includes* moral, and thus experiential or existential, judgment. (This is of course true of all the Bible's wisdom literature.)

We may also note here that *epignosis*, "full knowledge," is a compound form of the noun *gnosis*, the common Greek word for knowledge, commonly used as such in the N.T. (for example, Rom 11:33; 15:14; 1 Cor 8:1; 13:8; Eph 3:19; Phil 3:8; Col 2:3; 2 Pt 3:18). Paul speaks of "the love of Christ that surpasses knowledge (*gnoseos*)" (Eph 3:19), and says similarly, "Love never ends. . . . as for knowledge, it will come to an end" (1 Cor 13:8).

From such references it is clear that "knowledge" in this sense is what we commonly mean by the word in English—rational understanding. Further, this word is also used in the sense of the knowledge of Christ. We may conclude therefore that a rational understanding of the basics of the Christian faith *is* a possibility, at least to a certain point (that is, *validly* but not *exhaustively*). Certainly we cannot arbitrarily make a radical disjunction between "knowledge" as rational knowledge and "full knowledge" as existential or experiential knowledge—this is grammatically impossible.

We must conclude then that Paul's prayer for wisdom and revelation "in the knowledge of him" at least includes the possibility of a rational, intellectual grasp of the Christian faith.

Notice the word *know* (vs 18)—Paul says, "that . . . you may know what is the hope," etc. Here again the Greek word (*eidenai*) cannot arbitrarily be limited to subjective existential knowledge but also may (and it does in some of its N.T. parallels) refer to rational knowledge.

b. *That such growth in wisdom and revelation includes increasing intellectual or rational knowledge of the faith is also suggested by the parallel with 1:9; God "has made known to" us in all wisdom and insight "the mystery of his will."* Without going into an analysis of the two words here (*sofia kai phronesei*), we can affirm the implicit union of rational and existential knowing in these words.

2. **We should note however that Paul is not *primarily* concerned that his hearers become increasingly rationally enlightened**

concerning God's plan. Without denying the rational element, we must affirm that *Paul's principal concern* was that Jesus' followers should reach "maturity, to the measure of the full stature of Christ" (4:13), or "become mature, attaining to the whole measure of the fullness of Christ" (TNIV, which has the virtue of highlighting the key term *fullness*).

This accent on maturity or full "humanhood" is clear from the objects of the verb "know." Paul prays that the Christians may know the hope to which they are called; the riches of their inheritance; and the immeasurable greatness of God's power. This is existential knowledge in the best sense—knowledge grounded in the experience of spiritual growth and reality.

3. **Finally, we return to the affirmation of the implicit unity of knowledge, and of the human capacity to know, which we encounter here and always in the Bible.** The human person is a unity. Distinctions between one's capacity for rational knowledge and for existential knowledge can be made only arbitrarily and artificially, for purposes of analysis. In fact, the human person is "one," and in this sense, his or her knowledge is "one." That a person can "know" something "objectively" without his or her subjective participation is a logical impossibility, as various authors have shown.[8]

We will therefore assume throughout this discussion the unity of knowledge and the unity of humankind (human personhood) and the possibility of a rational knowing—valid, but not exhaustive—the basic truths of God and his dealing with humans.

---

[8] See for example Robert Blaikie, *"Secular Christianity" and God Who Acts* (Grand Rapids: Eerdmans, 1970).

1:18 — The hope to which he has called you.

The word "hope" occurs only four times in Ephesians (1:12; 1:18; 2:12; 4:4), compared with eight times for " faith" and 20 for "love." This tends to confirm what Paul implies in 1 Corinthians 13, that hope is the "third greatest thing" in the kingdom of God. Hope is important—crucially important in fact in the church's kingdom mission— and is of course related to faith. But hope can never be considered as equal to or in practice superseding faith, as appears to happen in Jürgen Moltmann's *Theology of Hope*.

Paul speaks here of "the hope to which he has called you" and in 4:4 of " the one hope of your calling"—that is, the hope embedded in your call. This hope is first of all the assurance through faith of our resurrection and eternal life with Christ. But in light of Ephesians 1:10 and similar passages, clearly it is also our hope for the uniting, reconciling of all things in Jesus Christ—the kingdom of God come in fullness.

1:19-20 — According to the working of his great power [which] God put to work in Christ when he raised him from the dead.

Paul states it clearly and leaves no doubt as to his meaning: God decisively, visibly showed his power by raising Jesus Christ from the dead. It happened—as an *act* of God (not just an "event") in which God showed himself powerful. Further, this power visible in the resurrection of Jesus Christ is the same power now at work in "us who believe." The resurrection becomes the cornerstone of our faith, not only in that it completes the necessary work of redemption, but that it proves God powerful to work in us, giving us assurance that he will in fact work powerfully in our lives and give us all things.

1:20-23 — *And seated him at his right hand in the heavenly places . . .*

Paul returns to God's cosmic plan or economy, further emphasizing and elaborating it (see the later discussion on 3:9-10). The exaltation of Christ occurs "not only in this age but also in the age to come." Here is unity of past, present, and future; of time and eternity, in Jesus Christ, who is the cosmic perspective and a reminder of "all things" (Eph 1:10).

Head over all things for the church, which is his body (1:22-23): here for the very first time in this letter Paul specifically mentions the church as "church" (*ekklesia*) and identifies it as the body (*soma*) of Christ.

It is noteworthy that this identification of the *church* as the *body of Christ* comes in the context of God's cosmic purpose. The church is more than merely the community of God's people on earth; it forms an integral part of God's plan for the ages, as we shall see. And the same Jesus Christ who is now "over all things" (vs 22) is also head of the church, his body.

Chapter 2

By Grace: Places Heavenly and Earthly

2:1 — As for you, you were dead in your transgressions and sins —

Paul's central point states that in Jesus Christ "you" (plural, the church) are now alive. You *were* dead; *now* you are alive. To accent this, some versions move the key action of verse 5 to verse 1, rendering it, "And you he made alive." Being made alive—conversion, regeneration, spiritual resurrection—is fundamental in all Paul is saying here.

2:2 — Following the course of this world, following the ruler of the power of the air, the spirit that is now at work among those who are disobedient —

"The course of this world" or to put it slightly differently, "the spirit of the age" refers to the standard for measurement reflected in the dominant course of society—what the majority felt and thought. "The prince of the power of the air" obviously refers to Satan; the idea seems to be that he is "the prince who rules over all that is called authority" (*Expositor's Greek Testament*). But why is he designated "prince" or "ruler of the power of the air"?

Satan was commonly referred to in Jesus' day as the "prince"

(KJV) or "ruler of devils" (Mt 9:34, 12:24; Mk 3:22), and Jesus several times called him "the ruler of this world" (Jn 12:31, 14:30, 16:11; here "world" is *kosmos*, the created universe). "The ruler of the power of the air" says essentially the same thing as "the prince of this world," though the emphasis is different. Satan is the *ruler* over all terrestrial powers to the extent that they have not yet been set at liberty in Jesus Christ. But Satan's sway is under the larger, higher sovereignty of Jesus Christ.

Interestingly, "world" — *kosmos* — appears in the preceding phrase, so that if "the course of this world" and the title "ruler of the power of the air" are to some extent parallel expressions, then we have here implicitly the idea of "the prince of this world." So "this world" and "powers of the air" are to some extent associated together.

Regarding "the power of the air": Adam Clarke says, "the *air* is supposed to be a region in which malicious spirits dwell, all of whom are under the direction and influence of Satan, their chief." This seems to have been the common idea in Paul's day, and thus of the early Christians. This idea presents no problem for today's Christians who recognize the fact of the existence of Satan and his evil hosts. Today we are inclined to think in more strictly immaterial terms of Satan and his angels, not putting them in some actual physical environment. Their environment is the spiritual world, we think, not literally "the air." But "powers of the air" serves to emphasize the inescapable presence of the powers of evil. Satan's accessibility to us can be limited only by the power and presence of the Holy Spirit, and perhaps our own character and will.

Biblical Christians most certainly will affirm the reality of Satan and his "powers of the air" while not necessarily thinking of these as literally inhabiting the physical atmosphere in the sense that fish live in water. On the other hand, some Christians may think Satan and his legions are so "spiritual" and immaterial that they have no real existence in the physical, material world. This is a mistake. We are still right now in the "heavenly places," even in our physical existence (as we saw earlier).

We will consider this further when we come to 6:12.

"The Spirit that is now at work among those who are disobedient." Those "having no hope and without God in the world" (2:12) are not living in freedom from the influence of spiritual powers. There is a spirit at work in them, Paul says: the spirit of Satan (which does not rule out the possibility of God's prevenient grace also influencing them). This contrasts sharply with 5:18, "Be filled with the Spirit." The big question: Which spirit will we serve? Which will work in us?

2:3 — All of us once lived among them —

This was the common human fate or condition. Specifically, by "all of us" Paul is including the Jews, showing that all shared the common need of salvation.

"Following the desires of flesh and senses" (or "body and mind" [RSV]) and living "in the passions of our flesh" is not limited to strictly body appetites; it includes as well the "desires of the senses," including the mind. Our rational capacity and processes are also affected by sin, so that the desires of our mind also tend toward evil.

2:4-6 — compare Romans 5:8, "But God proves his love for us in that while we were still sinners Christ died for us."

2:6 — raised us up with him and seated us with him in the

heavenly places in Christ Jesus —

This is the third occurrence of "the heavenly places." The reference here is back to 1:20-21. As God "raised [Jesus] from the dead and seated him at his right hand in the heavenly places," so he has "raised us up with him seated *us with him* in the heavenly places in Christ Jesus" (and the parallel continues, including the future, "the age to come" (1:21), or "the ages to come" (2:7). What is said of Christ is said of his disciples, those saved by him. What is true of the head is also true of the body (at least in this sense).

"Raised us up with him" clearly refers to resurrection, for he "made us alive together with Christ" (2:5), though dead. This is the spiritual resurrection from the death of sin to the life of God. However as S. D. F. Salmond notes, the verb here "expresses the definite idea of *resurrection*, and primarily that of physical resurrection. The introduction of this term and the following makes it not improbable that both ideas, that of the present moral resurrection and that of the future bodily resurrection, were in Paul's mind, and that he did not sharply distinguish between them, but thought of them as being one great gift of life" (*Expositors Greek Testament*). In a sense Paul's vision here transcends time; the moral and the physical resurrection are all one to him. This is consistent with what to us may seem the rather peculiar idea that we *now* share in "the heavenly places" with our Lord. (See note on 1:3).

2:7 — *in the ages to come* —

Paul speaks of "this age" and "the age to come" (1:21), and says we were chosen by God "before the foundation of the world" (1:4). Obviously this is no mere distinction between past, present, and future. Rather, there was that period of time, or "pre-time," before God created the world. There is also the past historical development leading up to Christ, who came in "the fullness of time" (1:10; cf. 3:5; 3:9). We are now in this present age, which will terminate (presumably with the return of Christ), bringing in the coming new age.

2:7 — that . . . he might show the immeasurable riches of his grace in kindness toward us in Christ Jesus —

The future in Christ is good and joyful; we have God's promise. We don't know the totality of all God will do "in the ages to come." But for those who are in Christ it will be something incomparably good, beyond "all that we can ask or imagine" (3:20).

2:8-9 — For by grace you have been saved through faith, and this is not your own doing; it is the gift of God — not the result of works, so that no one boast —

Here in the midst of Paul's discussion of the supremacy of Jesus Christ and his plan for the church we find this most remarkable and important word concerning the nature of personal salvation. This declaration is important in itself but even more profound in the context of Paul's larger argument.

This concise statement is not only a revelation of God's truth; it is also a remarkably precise doctrinal statement. Life in Christ *is* essentially *life*; doctrine is distinctly secondary. But life in Christ, as revealed by God, is of such a nature that true statements can be made describing this life and the way in which one enters into it. The supreme personal God here reveals himself (as for that matter all through the Bible) in statements or declarations or "propositions."

Paul specifically points to the following facts about our salvation:

1. It is by grace. Paul has already cited God's grace several times. It is "glorious grace" which God "freely bestowed on us in the Beloved" (1:6); his grace which "he lavished upon us" (1:8). Now Paul repeats what he said in 2:5, "by grace you have been saved."

> a. *Our salvation is thus totally of God's initiative.* By God's merciful acts providing redemption through Jesus Christ we live in a world governed by grace. Thanks to God's great love for us, even though we live in a world in a limited sense governed by sin and Satan, yet higher and broader than Satan's dominion is the circle or sphere of God's grace. God has surrounded his whole sinful creation by grace! Thus our situation can be depicted graphically as follows:

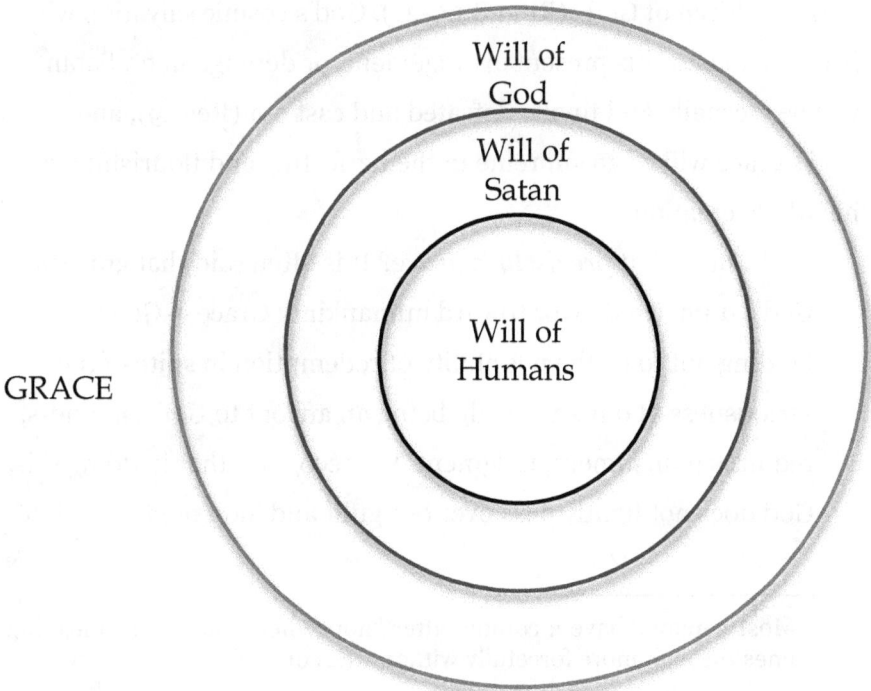

GRACE

Will of
God

Will of
Satan

Will of
Humans

Think of these as concentric spheres. Humans inhabit a sphere of action in which persons are free to act — to accept or reject God — *within the limits of* that sphere. Yet the whole sphere of human life on earth is within the sphere of Satan's dominion. Satan has awesome power in the world and over people and all human society. But what the Christian recognizes by biblical revelation and the Holy Spirit is that *Satan's sphere of action is also limited.* It is totally within the sphere of God's grace, of God's will. God has permitted this situation to exist *temporarily*, for the present time only; "for the creation was subjected to futility, not of its own will but by the will of him who subjected it in hope";[9] for the will of God is sovereign, and even this "futility" exists within the all-encompassing circle of God's grace, for "the creation itself will be set free from its bondage to decay and obtain the freedom of the glory of the children of God" (Rom 8:20-21). God's cosmic salvation will bring to an end this present arrangement, or derangement. Satan will be eternally and finally defeated and cast out (Rev 19), and God's grace will reign supreme in the perfecting and flourishing of his whole creation.

b. *But what precisely is grace?* It is often said that grace is God's unmerited favor toward humankind. Grace is God's holding out to us the possibility of redemption in spite of the seriousness of our sin which, being an affront to God's holiness, requires punishment, judgment. We recognize that in doing this, God does not lightly pass over our guilt and judgment-

---

[9] Most versions have a comma after "hope" here, but Paul's meaning comes through more forcefully without the comma.

worthiness, because Jesus Christ took upon himself the curse of our guilt by his death on the cross.

All this is true, but grace means much more. In these passages several aspects of what grace is can be seen.

1) *Grace is God's taking the initiative in providing salvation, and God's actual accomplishing of this salvation.* Paul states this forcefully and unequivocally— "you were dead," "we were dead"! (2:1, 5). But God made us alive. We were dead, and as the dead cannot rise to life of themselves—all possibility of initiative has gone—so the possibility of saving ourselves was completely gone.

But God accomplished resurrection. "God, who is rich in mercy, out of the great love with which he loved us even when we were dead through our trespasses, made us alive together with Christ" (2:4-5). To leave no room for doubt, Paul adds, "this is not your own doing; it is the gift of God" (2:8).

2) *Grace, as a moral attribute of God, specifies the way in which God reveals himself in his relation to humankind.* God shows himself loving and kind by his gracious acts—by dealing with us not as we deserve, but on the basis of his love and kindness—his character.

3) *Thus grace, like love, is strictly a relationship word.* It implies purpose, and therefore personality. Only a God who is personal could be said to be gracious.

4) *Also, grace is not some quality that exists independently of God.* God has acted; God has revealed himself, and in a way that we as persons perceive to be for our own good. To this merciful self-disclosure of God we

apply (and God himself applies in Scripture) the word "grace."

Beyond the fact that salvation is by grace, Paul notes:

2. Salvation is through faith. This is emphasized not only here, but elsewhere in the letter. The Gentiles who have "believed in him" have been saved (1:13). Paul speaks of "your faith in the Lord Jesus" (1:15) and of God's power "for us who believe" (1:19). Our access to God is "through faith in him" (3:12). Christ dwells "in your hearts through faith" (3:17).

So here we have the mystery—almost a paradox—of God's part and our part in salvation; God's grace and our faith prompted by the Spirit. Biblically we dare not fall off into either side of this mystery, trying to resolve it *either* by making salvation to be so entirely God's working that our response in faith is either unnecessary or predetermined, *or* by understanding salvation to be so entirely by our faith that the mystery of God's grace and the working of his Spirit are annulled. The fact is that salvation is *by grace, through faith* — by God's grace, freely given (by the free act of a personal God), and by our faith, freely exercised (as the free act of a personal being created by God, enabled by prevenient grace).

The mystery and the paradox involved here will not seem quite so impossible if we remember what has previously been said about the human sphere of action (which is finite) and God's sphere of action (which is infinite). Biblically we must maintain that within his sphere, which God has established, *man and woman really are free.* But it is a limited freedom, because the sphere of human action is totally within the sphere of God's grace, of the divine will. God "invades" the sphere of human action with the offer of salvation and with the divine mystery of the prevenient operation of his Holy

Spirit. But within this freedom persons may accept or reject this offer. They may accept through faith and be "made alive," or reject it, condemning themselves to eternal judgment.

Faith is saying "yes" to God. It is taking God at his word; believing that, when God promises something, he most assuredly will do it (Rom 4). Specifically, the faith that brings us into a relationship with God through Jesus Christ by the Spirit is our acceptance of this offer of salvation. It is also our agreeing with God and his evaluation of our sinful condition and need for rescue and our casting aside of any hope for liberation in any source other than Jesus Christ. Therefore an *acceptance* of Jesus Christ as Savior and a *covenant commitment* to live according to his will and commandments is an end result.

Faith thus is essentially an act of the will, a decision to accept God's offer and a decision to believe. The moment we sincerely *will* to accept God's rescue—which means recognizing our own sinfulness in repentance before God—we are saved in the essential initial sense that God makes us alive and we pass from death into life.

3. This is not our own doing. "This" may possibly refer either to "faith" or to salvation in general. It appears more natural to refer it not narrowly to faith; rather it is the fact of our salvation, our divine rescue, that is the gift of God and thus not of our own doing. (So write both Calvin and Wesley.)

Our salvation is not our own doing; not our "good work." Although we are saved through faith, it is not our faith which accomplishes our redemption; it is God. Only God can save in this fundamental resurrection sense. Clearly salvation is much more than a subjective experience caused by the salutary psychological effects of believing and commitment. Psychologically ("existentially"), anyone may be "converted" to any cause by faith and commitment to it (as many have been "genuinely converted" to Communism, Capitalism, Scientism, and many other isms). This "conversion" may be thorough and genuine in terms of its effects on our minds and hearts and behaviors. In such cases a person may in fact be "made alive" in the sense of having new energy, purpose, and direction. Such a conversion may produce changes which are psychologically similar (or even equivalent) to Christian conversion because the same psychological and personality factors are at work. But theologically and objectively in the true biblical kingdom-of-God sense, only God can save, rescue, liberate, make alive, fill with divine love.

A person genuinely converted to God through Christ exercises faith; and this faith, as personal act, produces certain effects in the person who believes. This act of faith is "conversion" (in the narrow sense), but becomes "regeneration" (and so, really salvation, liberation, transformation) only as God actually does forgive the person and make him or her "a new humanity" (3:15) by the power of the Holy Spirit who imparts "the divine nature" (2 Pt 1:4).

Thus on the human side it naturally follows that:

(a) A person may have a "religious experience" in which he or she is in some sense changed; they may be "converted," but this conversion may be spurious in the Christian sense. It may be a conversion *to* a particular person, a false religion or an ideology, a "Christian" cult, and so forth. But if it is not truly faith in Christ, the person has not really experienced Christian conversion. God has not forgiven him or her, and they are still in their sins, despite their (perhaps real, profound, and undeniable) "religious" (or "primary," or "first order") experience.

(b) It also follows that Christian conversion can be fully (or almost fully) explained psychologically (or even, from a different perspective, sociologically), so far as what takes place within the person as psychological (or sociological) being is concerned. This can be a completely valid analysis. It becomes invalid only when it asserts that a human being is *only* a psychological (or sociological, or whatever) being.

Actually what has been explained in this case (perhaps validly, perhaps not) is merely the working of one aspect of human personality. Psychology cannot deal with — does not in fact have the tools to deal with — the question of whether God has, in fact, entered the picture, whether what has happened is *merely* a particular psychological function, or whether a transcendental action and purpose was at work. For psychology (as well as traditional other sciences) cannot, on its traditional presuppositions, investigate the possibility of truly purposeful action, either human or divine.[10]

(c) It naturally follows also that on the "subjective" (so-called) and purely psychological side, Christian conversion can be counterfeited. That is, an experience psychologically equivalent (or in many respects equivalent) to true Christian conversion can be produced in a person through psychological manipulation. This can happen either by calculated intention, as in the case of Communist "brainwashing" in the 1950s and

---

[10] Blaikie, *"Secular Christianity" and God Who Acts* is clear on this point.

1960s, or in other ways, as in some highly emotional cults, false religions, and other mass movements. It can happen through a "technology of behavior," as once proposed by psychologist B. F. Skinner in his best-selling *Beyond Freedom and Dignity*.[11]

But when it comes to true Christian conversion, we are face to face with the operation of Almighty God: "this is not your own doing."

4. It is the gift of God — as is clear by what has already been said. The distinction is radical: "*you* were dead." But God acted: "you *he* made alive." God "raised us up." "For the wages of sin is death, but the free gift of God is eternal life through Jesus Christ our Lord" (Rom 6:23).

a. That salvation is a *gift* emphasizes that it is unmerited; it is by grace.

b. Being a gift, it therefore cannot be earned, but only accepted by faith. The human person's part comes in precisely here: one may accept by faith, or may refuse the gift, which is refusing to believe. Grace is not "irresistible" in the sense that God gives the gift to someone who refuses to accept or believe.

5. Not the result of works, so that no one may boast. The gift is not given because of what we have done. It cannot be earned. It remains a free gift.

While we are expecting to be justified before God on the basis of what we do, we are making the most fundamental of errors: our faith is really in *ourselves*, not in Jesus Christ. Salvation by works is really self-centered and egoistic; it is proof of the fact that we are

---

[11] B. F. Skinner, *Beyond Freedom and Dignity* (New York: Alfred A. Knopf, 1971).

still in sin, still seeing things from the sinful human's point of view, not from God's. For justification is nothing if it is not precisely this: *giving up* all idea that we can save ourselves; accepting God's point of view and God's evaluation of our condition; recognizing that our sin is so serious that only Christ's atonement is sufficient to remove it as an obstacle between us and God.

"So that no one may boast." Boasting is the opposite extreme of the attitude a person must have to receive the gift — an attitude of sorrow for sin, repentance, contrition — all the more so as we recognize *the supreme value of the gift* and our own utter unworthiness to receive it.

2:10 — *for we are what he has made* [RSV: *his workmanship*], *created in Christ Jesus for good works, which God prepared beforehand to be our way of life* [RSV: *that we should walk in them*] —

Paul is quick to point out the proper place of good works. Salvation is "not because of works," but the saved are "created . . . *for* good works." A strong statement. There is no saving value in our good works, but it is God's will that we *do* good works.

Indeed we are made by God, saved by him, *in order that* we may do good works. Part of God's purpose in saving us is that good works should be done. From the biblical perspective then, salvation without works is not complete salvation, as the letter of James makes clear.

Further, these good works "God prepared beforehand." This, not in the sense of predetermining human acts, but in the sense of the *preexisting plan of God* which God is bringing to realization through saving men and women and through the works they subsequently do. (In other words, we see the works of the kingdom, which Jesus began and continues through his body by the Spirit).

So here we encounter again this fact of *God's plan* and *God's purpose*. We are saved not only for our own sake, but because there are specific things — "works" — which God in his plan wishes to accomplish, and he wishes and intends to accomplish these through the activity of those who are saved.

But who are those who are saved, if not the church? This precisely is Paul's theme: What God is doing through the church. This *is* "the plan of the mystery hidden for ages in God who created all things, so that through the church the wisdom of God in its rich variety [or colors] might now be made known . . ." (3:9-10), and made known to a significant and essential degree by the *works* of those who are members of the church. What we see are the acts of Christ's body.

But there is more here. God has prepared these works beforehand. That is, it is already in the mind and plan of God that certain things — certain works, which are part of the overall plan which God is accomplishing — should be actually done by the church, as "good works." Thus human beings, redeemed, share in the realization of God's cosmic plan. That which God has set about to do since the creation of the world (which we have seen is "to unite all things in [Christ], things in heaven and things on earth") is in part to be accomplished by the good works of those who are saved and live by grace. Thus God's plan is, to some extent and in some sense, to be accomplished "through the church."

We will need to study this more in connection with 3:9-10. What are these good works? How do they fit into God's cosmic plan? What do they have to say concerning the relationship between the mission and structure of the church? For apparently there is a relationship.

The important phrase here is that these good works "God prepared beforehand." This clearly ties good works to God's cosmic plan (a central theme of Ephesians). It indicates that this statement is much more than just a general call to do good works, as though the importance were totally in the doing. It is important, according to this passage, not merely that the church do good works, but that the church do specifically those good works which God prepared beforehand, those works which are part of his cosmic plan.

God has in effect "subcontracted" a part of his cosmic plan to the church, so it is strategically important that the church actually fulfill that part of the plan. God subcontracts this part of his plan to the church, not merely so that the saved may demonstrate the reality of their salvation by good works, but that God's plan may be actually be fulfilled. The significance is not alone in the existential meaning of the works for the believer, but more in the objective fact of the fulfilling of God's plan. So it is important that we try to discover, as we study the unfolding of God's plan in Ephesians, the terms of the contract. What is it specifically that God wants us to do? Which good works actually help to carry out God's cosmic plan?

I use the words *contract* and *subcontract* above, but actually the proper biblical word here is *covenant*. This is not a cold business agreement, but a relationship.

Note: ". . . that we should walk in them" (RSV), or "to be our way of life" (NRSV). Not, "that we should do good works," but "that we should walk in them." Later in Ephesians Paul stresses the importance of Christians' *walk* —their daily manner of life. We are to "walk in love" (5:2 KJV), "as children of light" (5:8); we are to walk "not as unwise people but as wise, making the most of the time" (5:15-16) being filled with the Spirit.

So the Christian is to walk in love; to walk in good works; to walk in the Spirit (Gal 5:16). In reality these three cannot be separated. Whoever walks in the Spirit walks in good works, for the works are the expression of the love the Spirit gives. They are the works of the Spirit through us.

Walking *in* good works suggests, then, that these works are the expression of a life. These works, which God has foreordained or planned in advance for us, are the natural daily expression of our life in Christ.

2:11-13 — We find a fourfold contrast here between the situation of the Gentiles before and after their conversion to Christ. Before their conversion the Gentiles were:

1. Separated from Christ (2:12).

2. Alienated from God's people (2:12).

3. Strangers to the promises (2:12).

4. Without hope, without God (2:12) .

But now in Christ they are:

1. Joined to Christ (2:13).

2. Part of God's people, fellow-citizens and members of the household (2:19).

3. Partakers of the promise (2:19).

4. With God, with hope (2:13, 16, 18).

This whole chapter presents a strong contrast between persons who do not know Jesus Christ as Savior and persons who do. In 2:1-10 it is noted that all (and not only Gentiles here, in contrast to 2:11-22, where Paul is specifically referring to Gentiles) who are without

Christ share the following situation:

1. Dead in sin (2:1).

2. Following the prince of the power of the air (Satan) (2:2).

3. Living in the passions of body and mind (2:3).

4. By nature, living as children of wrath (2:3).

"But God" (2:4) changed the situation, so that now, through faith in Christ:

1. We are made alive (2:5).

2. Made followers of Jesus Christ, who was raised up to the place of power (contrast with Satan) (2:5-6).

3. Made to sit with him in the heavenly places, that we might know the immeasurable riches of his grace (2:6-7).

4. Reconciled to God, making us (implicitly here) his sons and daughters (2:5-6, 19).

2:12 — *You were at that time separated from Christ, alienated from the commonwealth of Israel —*

Here Paul (fittingly, in the light of his theme) ties personal salvation to the church in the sense that to be without Christ is to be alienated from God's people. This emphasizes the fact that salvation is more than the establishing of a right relationship between God and humans. It is also the becoming part of God's people, the church. This fact must continually be emphasized. Our goal is to see people saved *and brought into the communion of God's people,* where the work of salvation continues and grows. Evangelism (in the sense of conversions or initial commitments to Jesus Christ) and church building ("edification") go together. Because of individualistic and other tendencies within much of Christianity, this connection must be self-consciously maintained. Evangelism in the biblical sense necessarily means incorporation into the Christian community—body of Christ embodiment.

2:12 — *Strangers to the Covenants of Promise* —

This phrase signals an important theological understanding of the Old Testament. Paul understood how the theological roots of the gospel developed through salvation history. Throughout Ephesians and other writings, Paul is working mostly off the Old Testament, showing how the Good News fulfills its prophecies and foreshadowings while simultaneously profoundly contextualizing the Good News to the Greco-Roman context.

2:14 — *For he is our peace* —

God is the God of peace; Jesus Christ *is* our peace, our *shalom*. Peace is the fruit of reconciliation; it is the sign that the separation, the struggle, or the conflict has ceased. Peace is a particularly Christian quality. It is based on the only possible way of reconciliation between God and humans, and between and among people, within persons internally, and within the larger "all things" context. Here of course Paul is speaking particularly of reconciliation between Jew and Gentile through Christ. Jesus brings peace—with all the depth of meaning that *shalom* and related terms bring with them from the Old Testament.[12]

2:14 — *Has broken down the dividing wall, that is, the hostility between us* —

This "dividing wall" is nothing less than "the law with its

---

[12] Further elaborated in Snyder and Scandrett, *Salvation Means Creation Healed.*

commandments and ordinances." That which separated Jew and Gentile was not sin (as the Jew might be tempted to think), for both—all—are sinners. Indeed, knowledge of sin comes by the law (Rom 5). What divided Jew and Gentile had been nothing less than the law, which Christ abolished "in his flesh." This law, symbolized by circumcision, "which is made in the flesh by human hands" (2:11), Christ abolished "in his flesh" by crucifixion.

2:15 — *That he might create in himself one new humanity* —

This is the new creation in Christ: one new humanity, the basis of the new community, the new Israel, the new being which is the body of Christ. Note: Paul's theme here is the church, the body of Christ. But the basis of the church is a human—Jesus Christ—and thus new men and women are persons made new by Jesus Christ.

Here again is a warning not to slight or slip over the fact of *personal, particular conversion* in our haste to emphasize the collective, communal aspects of the church. The church begins with the "new human"— from which then it becomes something much more than the mere accumulation of numerous "new people" or "saved individuals"—for it is indeed the body of Christ. It is a new entity, more than the mere sum of its parts, a new social reality — first, because it is the habitation of the Holy Spirit, the body of Christ; and also because (both sociologically and spiritually) the uniting of persons into a community organization, or institution, always produces a new being. This entity has a real existence, which while not independent from its constituents, is made new. So again: The church is a social, a spiritual, and a sociological reality. All these dimensions together make up the church's ecology.

Who is this "new man," this new human person? Any person

who has been forgiven and redeemed through the blood of Christ (1:7), who has been made alive (2:1ff), who has been saved by grace through faith (2:8). Given what Paul has already said in this letter, it is clear that there can be no other basis for the "new humanity," and hence no other foundation for the new community, the church. Yet Paul always has in view here the community (the corporate humanity) as well as particular people.

2:15 — *One new humanity in place of the two* —

Reconciliation. The hostility is at an end; peace has come. Paul is talking about reconciliation between Jew and Gentile through Christ, but this reconciliation includes the reconciliation of all disruptive differences between humans, as is made plain elsewhere in the New Testament—be they social, cultural, sexual, ethnic, or economic. Further, as we have seen, the reconciliation Jesus has brought and is bringing includes cosmic reconciliation.

2:16 — *And might reconcile both groups to God in one body through the cross* —

Jesus' death was one of mediation and expiation—dealing with the fact and power of sin. His death on the cross effects a real and "experience-able" reconciliation between holy God and sinful humans. Thus in Christ there is horizontal reconciliation ("us both") and vertical reconciliation ("to God") That is: I find reconciliation with my believing brother and sister because we both are reconciled to God. We are kin, family, not first of all because God has made us sisters and brothers, but because God has become Father to both of us. Hence we are now part of the same family.

"Body" is a big word in the Ephesian letter. It has already

appeared in 1:23, referring to the church, "which is his body."

Does "in one body" here refer to Christ's physical body which died on the cross, or to the church as the body of Christ? Commentators and exegetes have differed on this point. But is it necessarily one or the other, exclusively? "Both to God in one body" suggests the new creation, the Christian community, while "through the cross" reminds us of Jesus' physical body which died and rose again. Perhaps here we have (consciously or unconsciously in Paul's mind) a profound transition from that physical, flesh-and-blood body which died but rose again, to the new creation (the church, body of Christ), which exists only because that physical, flesh-and-blood body really did die and rise again in space, time, and history.

"Through the cross" reminds us of the supremely high cost of this reconciliation. A reconciliation which required death, and not just my death, but the death of the only Son of God (Jn 3:16)—the only one who could effect this reconciliation, being both God and a one-hundred-percent human person.

2:18 — *For through him we both have access in one Spirit to the Father* —

The unity —one new person (or humanity), one body, one Spirit, the oneness of God's plan —begins to emerge.

The presence here of specific references to Jesus Christ ("him"), the Father, and the Spirit, is striking. Whether this Trinitarian aspect was consciously present in Paul's mind or not is immaterial. Biblical writers under the inspiration of the Holy Spirit often wrote more than they knew or intended! Certainly the Holy Spirit knew what he was doing, and we may properly consider this statement as a biblical evidence of the fact of the Trinity.

Through Christ we have access to the Father in one Spirit. God has made himself available to us; the expiation of Jesus Christ has opened the way directly to God. We are now members of the family, as the veil has been removed. "The Spirit you have received is a Spirit that makes us sons [and daughters], enabling us to say 'Abba! Father!' In that cry the Spirit of God joins with our spirit in testifying that we are God's children" (Rom 8:15-16 NEB).

In the words "through him we both have access in one Spirit to the Father" (2:18) we see again how truly our salvation is "by grace," "the gift of God." *It is God* in the person of Jesus Christ who opens access to himself through the death on the cross. *It is God* in the person of the Holy Spirit who acts in our hearts to convince and convict us and draw us to place our faith in this work of Christ. And *it is God* the Father with whom we now have direct communion because of this work of Son and Spirit.

The Tri-Personal God acts in personal ways to bring us to himself. So we see here also the harmonious operation of each Person of the Holy Trinity.

2:19 — *So then you are no longer strangers and aliens* —

We are no longer strangers in the sense of being alienated from God and his people; no longer aliens or sojourners wandering aimlessly, lost, in our own sins. The emphasis is on alienation and the need for reconciliation. Those once separated (especially and specifically here, the Gentiles) have now been made a part of the people of God.

Yet it remains true that this "people of God," the church, is a pilgrim people, wandering (although led by God) in a hostile world with which we will always be in tension (Heb 11:13-16, 1 Pt 2:11).

Whoever is part of the household of God is a sojourner on the earth; whoever is totally at home and reconciled to the things of this world is a stranger to God's people. Peace with God and with our believing sisters and brothers often brings trouble in the world.

2:19 — *members of the household of God* (Greek *oikeioi*, "household" or "family") —

In this passage the church is pictured as a building (2:14-22). But this is no static conception. It begins with the idea of the household of God, and the construction itself is conceived of as dynamic and growing. Here the church is not so much the *body* of Christ as "a *holy temple* in the Lord" (vs 21). But the position and function of Jesus is parallel to that in the image of body: Head of the body, chief cornerstone of the building.

2:20 — *built upon the foundation of the apostles and prophets* —

Historically, as the means through which God revealed himself and prepared the way for the church, and also in the sense of apostolic teaching. In another sense, Jesus Christ himself is the foundation.

2:21 — *a holy temple* —

The biblical images of temple and tabernacle have considerable relevance for ecclesiology, especially in relation to church structure. Both the Old Testament concepts of temple and tabernacle find their fulfillment *in the church as the body of Christ*, so that there can no longer be an actual, physical temple for the church in the sense of a holy place. Like the Old Testament priesthood and sacrifices, the actual, material tabernacle and temple have been fulfilled in Jesus Christ and in the church and have thus passed away (cf. Jn 4:20-24, Heb 8 and 9).[13]

2:22 — *built together spiritually into a dwelling place for God —*

More literally: "a dwelling in which God lives by his Spirit" (NIV). It is the Holy Spirit of God who inhabits the temple—just as in the Old Testament tabernacle and temple. This is true now—*fulfilled*—in the Holy Spirit's indwelling the church and each believer.

Here again the implicit Trinitarian dimension of these two verses (2:21-22) is notable.

---

[13] I discuss this in some detail in *The Problem of Wineskins,* Chapter 4, "Churches, Temples, and Tabernacles."

Chapter 3

The Mystery of God's Plan

God's plan in and through the church is a "mystery" or "secret" (*musterion*) in the biblical sense. This Paul explains in chapter three of Ephesians.

3:2 — *The stewardship of God's grace* (RSV) —

This is a key phrase in Ephesians. It should be compared with 1 Peter 4:10, which speaks of being "good stewards of the manifold grace of God." Paul again uses the word *oikonomia* here, so the phrase may be translated "the economy of God's grace." Since *oikonomia* has a range of meanings, various English versions use a range of words here: stewardship, commission, administration, dispensation. In contemporary English, the best terms for Paul's meaning here are *stewardship* and *economy*. Certainly *commission* fits the context, but Paul's ministry was more than a commission. It was a stewardship—to be a good steward of God's plan of salvation.

God's grace *is* a stewardship, and not just for Paul. Receiving and accepting God's grace places *responsibility* on the recipient. There is such a thing as our stewardship of the gospel message. Those who know Jesus Christ are like the servants given talents: God wants these used in such a way that they bear fruit. And God wants the gospel proclaimed *in such a way* that it brings results.

The commission is not merely to go and preach, but to produce results, fruit—to make disciples and raise signs of God's reign.

In Paul's case, this meant a particular commission and responsibility for the Gentiles. But he always had the gospel in its broadest scope in view, as we saw especially in Ephesians 1.

3:3 — *the mystery was made known to me by revelation* —

This is the claim, implicitly, of the whole Bible. What is written here is not a collection of human speculations about God. It is something revealed by God: Certain truths concerning his will, his character, and his acts in history which men and women have recorded, commented on, and (to a certain extent, and especially in the case of Paul) have analyzed and explained.

But here Paul speaks of "the mystery." What is this mystery? As we have seen, *mystery* is another key word in Ephesians. The mystery is, he says, that now "the Gentiles have become fellow heirs" (vs 6). In other words, the mystery is *the universality of the gospel*. The Good News, Paul has come to understand, is not exclusively for God's (historically) chosen people, but is now, through them, for everyone who will hear and accept. This came by particular revelation to Paul.

Paul emphasizes that this fact was not merely the conclusion of human reasoning. It was revealed "by the Spirit," to him, and the "apostles and prophets" of the early church (3:5).

3:9-11 — Now, however, we leave behind this somewhat narrower sense of mystery as God reveals to us through Paul "the plan of the mystery hidden for ages in God who created all things." This is none other than God's "eternal purpose" (3:11), which has been the basic theme of this epistle since its beginning, as we have noticed.

Paul has already indicated, in general, what this plan is: it is "to gather up all things in [Christ], things in heaven and things on earth" (1:10), to bring everything, all creation, under the proper headship of Jesus Christ. But now Paul gives fuller expression to this same thought, adding new elements: "the plan (*oikonomia*) of the mystery hidden for ages in God who created all things" is "that through the church the wisdom of God in its rich variety might now be made known to the rulers and authorities in the heavenly places" (vss 9-10).

This plan is to be realized—amazingly—through the church! But before we can ask *how* this may be, we must note *what it is* that God is accomplishing, the object of his action through the church. It is that "the wisdom of God in its rich variety might now be made known to the rulers and authorities in the heavenly places."

The rulers and authorities in the heavenly places —

This is a particularly difficult concept. Volumes have been written trying to explain what Paul and the Bible mean by "rulers and authorities" or "principalities and powers," as the phrase is often translated (KJV and others). The issue is compounded by the fact that Paul refers to principalities and powers "in the heavenly places."

Four main interpretations have been given to the "rulers and authorities" or "principalities and power" mentioned by Paul here and elsewhere in his writings (Rom 8:38; Col 1:16, 2:10, 15). In summary:

1. Some have taken these references to mean the *legions of demons and spirits* that were thought to inhabit and encircle the earth, especially dwelling in the air above the earth. These were thought to have considerable influence on human life. Sometimes they were associated with the various stars and planets and with the forces of nature.

There is some justification for such an interpretation if one takes into account extra-biblical literature of the first century. On the other hand, interpreting the Bible on the basis of extra-biblical literature is always questionable and can easily lead to some decidedly unbiblical conclusions. This has often happened in biblical studies, e.g., with relation to the Old Testament and ancient pagan mythology. If the Bible is truly a unique revelation from a personal God—the consistent position of orthodox Christian theology through the centuries—then it must be interpreted on its own terms. Thus "principalities and powers" must be taken to mean what the various biblical references seem to indicate, and not necessarily anything more.

2. A second, more traditional interpretation of the "principalities and powers" is that these represent in general *all unseen spiritual beings*, whether God's hosts of angels or the fallen angels which compose the kingdom of Satan. Among the Jews it was traditional to think of these as comprising a hierarchy of spiritual powers, and Paul may have thought of them in this way (see the comment on 1:3). For us today, this is not centrally important. The main fact here is the identification of the "principalities and powers" with the whole realm of spiritual beings created by God, whether holy or fallen.

Regardless of what else "principalities and powers" may refer to, it seems clear from the biblical use of the phrase that this is the most natural interpretation.

3. A third interpretation is to identify "principalities and powers"

with *earthly, temporal rulers.* Thus they mean kings and princes, governments and kingdoms. There is some biblical justification for this in that Paul speaks of submitting to rulers and authorities (i.e., principalities and powers) in a way that clearly suggests temporal government authority (e.g., Rom 13.1). But this earthly, temporal interpretation runs into problems with such passages as Ephesians 6:12, "not against enemies of blood and flesh, but against the rulers, against the authorities, against the cosmic powers of this present darkness, against the spiritual forces of evil in the heavenly places."

4. A modern variation of this interpretation has been to identify the principalities and powers not with human rulers but with the various *human institutions* that govern life. These are the sociological and cultural structures and macrostructures which, as sociology and cultural anthropology have shown, seem to have an existence in themselves almost independent of the human beings who create and operate them. These structures exert a real influence greater than the sum of their human parts. Thus "spirits" and "demons" can be dispensed with as elements of a bygone, premodern worldview, but these passages are still highly relevant sociologically.

The limitations of this view are obvious. Paul here obviously *is* speaking of some kind of real spiritual powers. Many other biblical passages speak similarly. Any interpretation which requires denying the clear sense of Scripture must be rejected as unbiblical. Whatever the sociological or psychological utility, any interpretation not consistent with the Bible properly understood ceases to be Christian theology.

What then can we legitimately say about "principalities and powers"? We should accept the most obvious and literal interpretation while also perceiving the new depth of meaning provided by disciplines such cultural anthropology, sociology, social psychology, and history.

Based on the full range of Scripture and church history to date, we can conclude the following three points:

1. In most cases, biblical references to "principalities and powers" indicate real created spirits which operate in and influence the world of people and culture. These include the heavenly spirits or angels that are in the service of Almighty God, his "heavenly hosts" (which may be organized in various hierarchies or divisions; we don't have much revelation about this).

More than 200 times the Old Testament refers to God as "Lord of hosts" or "Lord of armies." Clearly YHWH commands vast multitudes of spiritual beings which are mostly invisible to us but which appear at special strategic times in the economy of God. A dramatic and in a sense paradigmatic instance is found in 2 Kings 6:17. "Then Elisha prayed: 'O Lord, please open his eyes that he may see.' So the Lord opened the eyes of the servant, and he saw; the mountain was full of horses and chariots of fire all around Elisha."

These powers also include "Satan and his angels," all spiritual beings of whatever nature they may be, that are in rebellion against God and in the service of Satan. Again, we don't have extensive biblical revelation here, but we have enough to make it clear that, according to the Bible, they do really exist.

This then is the primary and most basic meaning of "principalities and powers."

These spiritual beings are active in the world of human experience and culture. This is true not in some mystical or magical or superstitious sense, as in paganism, but more directly, as forces which influence human behavior. The Bible speaks of Satan as implanting evil suggestions which produce ungodly behavior (Jn 13:27; Acts 5:3; 1 Cor 7:5; cf. Mk 1:13; 2 Cor 11:14). In Ephesians Paul mentions Satan several times (2:2, 4:27, 6:11, 16) and refers to him as "the ruler [or prince] of the power of the air, the spirit that is now at work among those who are disobedient" (2:2). It is clear from Scripture that Satan commands a host or army of fallen angels (or demons, or devils, or unclean spirits), and that these are responsible for or at least implicated in many human and social problems and sins. These spiritual beings include Paul's "messenger of Satan" (2 Cor 12:7), the evil one who takes away the good seed of the gospel (Lk 8:12), and of course the many forms of "demon possession" (as it is often called).

It may seem odd that anyone who really believes in the God of the Bible and in Jesus Christ who really was born, died, and rose again, would have difficulty accepting the fact of human oppression or possession by evil spirits. Man and woman were made to be "possessed by" (that is, filled with) the Holy Spirit. Usually people *will* be "possessed" by or obsessed with something or someone. If one truly believes in the fact of sin and therefore in the necessity of Christ's expiatory death and in the possibilities of the indwelling of the Holy Spirit, then biblically it is simply inconsistent to deny or doubt the fact of demon possession.

There is of course mystery here. We may not always be able to distinguish clearly for example between demon possession, mental illnesses, or various forms of erratic behavior. This is why the church needs the discerning work of the Spirit often given through the Spirit's gifts (discussed below in Ephesians 4).

2. It is possible that these spirits have or assume specific

63

functions in relation to human beings. The idea of "guardian angels" seems to have some support in the words of Christ (Mt 18:10), though the idea is often romanticized or sentimentalized well beyond biblical teachings. In the case of Satan's angels (which I take to be the same thing as "evil spirits" or "demons") it is not unthinkable that Satan would assign some spirits specific tasks or even specific human persons, just as an army general might assign units to specific tasks or to engage specific elements of the enemy. Something like this apparently happened in the case of Saul (1 Sam 16:14ff). The New Testament also gives various examples (e.g., Mt 15:22, Acts 19:13-16, etc.).

The idea that evil spirits directly influence particular people either through actual "possession" or in more subtle, less recognizable ways is not hard to believe when one reads of such men as Vladimir Lenin, Joseph Stalin, and especially Adolph Hitler. Hitler displayed a total perversity wholly consistent with the nature of Satan himself. This is evident in two of his characteristics, especially: his utter dishonesty whereby he consistently and consciously sought to deceive, saying just the opposite of his real intentions, and his deliberate and utterly senseless cruelty. Cruelty, persecution, torture, and murder became ends in themselves. In World War II for example provisions for the extermination camps were actually given priority over vital war materials and needs. This was actually suicidal, as is all evil, ultimately.

It is very easy in such cases to believe in demon possession. A man or woman can so open themselves to evil that Satan actually takes possession of the person through one or more of his fallen angels. Exactly *how* this happens, or what it means psychologically, we may never know. But history suggests that it does happen.

Short of what we generally call actual possession, such spirits are presumably at work among people in other ways. They may prompt or suggest evil thoughts and actions. They may come to us disguised as angels of light.

3. But now comes the question: *What is the operation of these spirits in relation to the structures of society?*

Sociologists and anthropologists point out that any social group or institution takes on a character of its own. It becomes more than the sum of its (human) parts. We speak of "team spirit" or "group spirit" to indicate a certain sense of supra-individual existence that such groups manifest. We say that "each church has its own personality," and it is true. Groups, *as groups*, as *corporate entities*, manifest characteristics which, to say the very least, in some ways parallel what we call human personality. (Note here the irony of the word "corporation." It literally means "embodied," an analogy from the human body.)

This corporate or supra-individual character is particularly true when we consider large human-made institutions. These may be business corporations, governments, denominations, universities, or even cities. *The institutional structure seems to take on an existence of its own.* It functions and makes decisions, for instance, that are not the decision—and at times, not even the desire—of any single person within the institution.

A pointed example here is the array of governmental decisions that lead a nation into war. Later historical analysis often reveals that it's a war no one really wanted. But who is responsible? How does one assign responsibility? When historians carefully research questions as to *who* made the key decisions, they often reveal a war no one wanted. Literally no one person or identifiable group of persons ever decided to (for example) go to war! *The institution decided.*[14]

But how can an institution, which has no will of its own, make decisions? Obviously an institutional decision is the cumulative result of the decisions of many individuals. But the "institutional mystery" is how these individual decisions add up to an institutional action that is contrary to the will of any of the decision makers. Sociologists, historians and economists point out "unintended consequences" of decisions.

All of this may seem a long way from biblical exegesis. As we shall see, really it is not. It is very much related to the problem of "principalities and powers."

Jacques Ellul (1912-1994), the prophetic French sociologist and lay theologian, wrote very insightfully on this subject in his 1970 book, *The Meaning of the City*. Ellul intentionally paired this theological study with his classic sociological analysis, *The Technological Society*.[15]

Ellul discusses the nature of the city *as a spiritual phenomenon.* According to Ellul, the city, "as a power, as a spiritual reality," is under God's curse. Ellul said "the city is an almost indistinguishable

---

[14] This is my reflection based on fairly wide reading over the years, and there is in fact a literature on this subject. Of course some wars have been very intentional and deliberate. Sometimes official declarations of war were made and can be documented. Yet even in cases like these the chain of events and influences that led to war is often murky and difficult to trace to specific persons and times. Additionally, often crucial decisions were affected or prompted by seemingly chance factors or events.

[15] Jacques Ellul, *The Meaning of the City* (Grand Rapids: Eerdmans, 1970); *The Technological Society* (New York: Knopf, 1970).

mixture of spiritual power and human work. It has a very definite spiritual character, an orientation toward evil and away from good which in no way depends on" human beings.

"The city has, then, a spiritual influence. It is capable of directing and changing a man's spiritual life." "Sociologists know that every city has its own personality," and this is spiritually significant. "We are dealing with a problem that is primarily spiritual." The city "is the second creation and wants autonomy. . . . She is her own reason for existing, in herself, a sufficient power, a sufficient law. It must be very clear that in his act of building, man gave birth to something stronger than himself. And it is neither the founder nor the inhabitants of the city who say so, but rather the city herself, in her personality independent both of men and of God. . . . I am, and no one else! This is not the proud statement of a man. This is the assertion of spiritual power, the affirmation of man's work which has gotten out of his hands and has claimed her own particular life."[16]

What precisely is meant when the city, or any other social institution, is described in these terms? To say that the city is a "spiritual power," that it has "personality" and a certain autonomy— what does this mean? Are these mere figures of speech? Metaphors for the mysterious power such institutions exhibit? Are we saying merely that the influence and "behavior" of the city are in some ways analogous to that of human beings? Or are we saying something more? In other words, does the city (for example) really possess a spiritual personality, or is this merely a figure of speech?

Ellul does not answer this question unequivocally. But he does

---

[16] Ellul, *Meaning of the City,* 164, 169, 9, 22, 52-53.

identify the spiritual power of the city with biblical references to "principalities and power."[17]

Ellul reminds us of the spiritual power of cities, of technology, and of all social institutions. What can we say biblically? Three things.

a. We note that "principalities and powers" refers not in the first instance to specific human beings but to "power structures," whether human or suprahuman.

b. We note that Paul is speaking not only of the heavenly, spiritual world, but also of the earthly, temporal world when he makes such references. God's plan to reconcile all things in Jesus Christ includes things "in this age" as well as in "that which is to come" (Eph 1:21). It is a uniting of "things in heaven *and* things on earth" (Eph 1:10).

Colossians 1:15-20 is uniquely significant and emphatic in this regard. Through Jesus Christ "all things *in heaven and on earth* were created, *things visible and invisible*, whether thrones or dominions or rulers or powers. . . . For in him all the fullness of God was pleased to dwell, and through him God was pleased to reconcile to himself all things, *whether on earth or in heaven.*"

c. The "rulers and powers" on earth include not only invisible powers but also visible ones. In other words, these passages clearly state that "principalities and powers" include (but are not limited to) *present, earthly, visible power structures.* What can these be, if not human institutions, the power structures of human society and culture?

---

[17] Ellul, *Meaning of the City*, 164ff.

We conclude then that "principalities and powers" means, in addition to the strictly spiritual or heavenly powers, human power structures, the various institutions which humans have created. These include governments, various societies and organizations, possibly also some church institutions, and especially (if we accept Ellul's thesis) the city and (by extension) nation states. All these are in addition to the invisible thrones and dominions, either in the service of God or of Satan, of which the Bible obviously speaks.

So when dealing with visible and invisible authorities and powers and their structures we are thinking both/and, not either/or. Both seem visible and invisible (to us), both on earth and in heaven.

But what of the precise spiritual nature of the earthly and visible authorities and powers? Are earthly power structures inhabited by those under the control of or otherwise influenced by spiritual beings? Can a city or organization or government be demon-possessed?

We are limited in what we can say because the Bible does not answer all our questions. However, the biblical record does teach us that *human institutions are not spiritually and morally neutral.* Precisely *how* they relate to spiritual forces we don't know. This may vary, as spiritual influences on particular persons vary. But the important fact is that *earthly institutions have spiritual significance* and influence. Human institutions are not morally neutral. In some sense and to some degree every human institution is under the influence either of God and his angels or of Satan and his forces of evil. And as there are spiritual battles for the control of persons, so there is spiritual warfare for the control of human institutions, whether governments, cities, corporations, universities, or churches. Perhaps even a city or other institution can become demon-possessed. Not that her inhabitants individually are, but that Satan is actually in complete or largely uncontested control of the spiritual being of the city. Such a city was Sodom.

So the city (to use this as an example) has spiritual significance. Is it, in itself, a spiritual being? Yes, in the sense that as a social institution, it exercises an influence that often is or seems to be autonomous. In addition, there may be "an angel of the city"—a spiritual being, good or evil, that inhabits or controls the city. On the other hand, the answer is no in the sense that the city is not *in and of itself* a spirit with self-consciousness and volition.

This, then, is what the New Testament means by "principalities and powers" or "rulers and authorities."

We can summarize all this in these points:

1. *"Principalities and powers" refers in general to the spiritual forces which influence human beings—whether visible or invisible, whether earthly or heavenly.*

2. *These include human institutions, all humanly created power structures which operate seemingly autonomously to influence human life* in ways that are morally and spiritually significant. These institutions are therefore spiritually important and arenas of spiritual warfare between God and Satan.

3. *We must guard against identifying "principalities and powers" exclusively with human institutions* however, precisely because the Bible doesn't. These powers include as well the invisible, strictly spiritual beings that also inhabit God's universe.

Returning to our text (Eph 3:9-11), we see that Paul here is speaking specifically about "the rulers and authorities in the heavenly places." What can this mean?

3:10 — in *the heavenly places* —

This is the fourth occurrence of this unusual phrase in Ephesians. As we have already seen, Paul uses it not in a local sense and certainly not in the sense of making a precise distinction between earth and heaven. This phrase signifies the totality of God's universe, both spiritual and material. As Christians we *are now in the heavenly places*, for we are within God's created world, which is both material and spiritual. As Christians we recognize this and remind ourselves of this essential truth.

Thus when Paul says God's plan is to make known the manifold wisdom of God to the rulers and powers in the heavenly places, this includes the principalities and powers on earth. The emphasis is not one of *locality* but of *essential nature*. The world, including physical matter, is essentially spiritual. It is in this world that God is operating through the church. (As we noted earlier, in the original Greek the word "places" does not occur; the phrase is simply "in the heavenlies.")

Here then we see the *sphere* of God's operation: the totality of God's universe, spiritually understood, including the material and immaterial creation. We see also the *objective* of God's operation: that his wisdom might be made known to the principalities and powers that inhabit and function within God's created order.

We are left then with this most amazing and startling phrase, "that *through the church* the wisdom of God in its rich variety might now be made known" in the heavenlies—that is throughout the universe!

3:10 — *through the church* —

Here we discover that God's eternal plan for his creation is to be accomplished in some essential sense and to some degree *through the church*. In other words, by the agency of the community of God's people. The question is, how? What does or can the church do to fulfill this amazing calling? Or is it that God simply uses the church as an inanimate object, a tool, to accomplish his purpose?

God does not use the church as an inanimate object. It is not a mere tool in his hands. That would conflict with everything he seeks to do *within* the church. God's will is that the church as a body and each member within it reach "maturity," "the measure of the full stature of Christ" (Eph 4:13). God's Spirit expects and prompts spiritual growth to maturity on the part of the church. As the church thus grows, it will accomplish God's plan to "through the church" make known "the wisdom of God in its rich variety to the rulers and authorities."

We have already noted the importance of 2:10 here. God's eternal plan for the church involves the "good works" which God "prepared beforehand" that those saved "by grace through faith" should perform, or "walk in" and be our way of life. In other words, what God is doing "through the church" is related to and in some measure accomplished by the church members' lives of good works.

So here we understand more fully how God is working *through the church*. Combining 2:10 and 3:10, we comprehend more fully God's plan. It is that through walking in good works, the church makes known the rich wisdom of God to the principalities and powers. What "good works" accomplish this? Specifically, those God "prepared beforehand," the works of Jesus, the works of the kingdom of God discerned day by day in and through the Christian community.

So this is God's plan: that the church in its life and work

participate strategically in his purpose to unite all things in Christ; to make known God's glory to the world's peoples and power structures, earthly or celestial.

This is not yet a full answer, however. We are still left with a big question. What specifically can and should the church do to fulfill this mind-boggling plan of God?

Let us continue on in Ephesians and see whether this question is answered.

3:11 — *This was in accordance with the eternal purpose that he has carried out in Christ Jesus our Lord* —

Jesus Christ remains central. It is *through him* that this eternal plan is being worked out and has already in fact been accomplished through the death, resurrection, and ascension of Jesus and the redemption thus provided (cf. 1:5-7, 2:4-7).

3:12 — *in whom we have access to God in boldness and confidence* —

Whatever it is that God is doing, we can be sure that the resources are adequate! We can have boldness and confidence of access to him and in him through Jesus by the Spirit.

3:14–19 — Paul's remarkable intercessory prayer in behalf of the (Ephesian) church. There is much here! Paul "bows [his] knees before the Father" and emphasizes that through him "every family in heaven and on earth takes its name." Once again the cosmic aspect! Once again we are dealing with heaven and earth—that is, the totality of God's creation, the field of operation of God's plan for the church.

Especially significant here in the light of God's eternal purpose for and through the church are the petitions Paul makes. His prayer is:

- that "you may be strengthened in your inner being with power through his Spirit;"
- "that Christ may dwell in your hearts through faith;"
- that you may be "rooted and grounded in love;"
- that you "may have the power to comprehend . . . what is the breadth and length and height and depth;"
- that you may "know the love of Christ that surpasses knowledge;"
- "that you may be filled with all the fullness Of God."

The verbs here are interesting: *strengthened, indwelt, comprehend, know, be filled.* Immediately we notice again the combination of intellectual or rational knowledge and heart experience, heart knowledge. We see the involvement of the total personality, the total human being, in the reality and experience of God's plan and concern expressed here through Paul's prayer.

Paul's prayer here certainly is in harmony with God's will. Thus it tells us more about God's plan for Christians—that is, for Jesus' body, the church. We see what God wishes to accomplish within the church and, consequently, we see additional aspects of God's eternal plan for the church.

Let's note more specifically what Paul is praying for here.

1. To be strengthened in your inner being with power through his Spirit —

"The *strengthening* was to take effect by means of *power imparted* or infused, and this impartation of power was to be made through the Spirit of God;" "a gift to enrich and invigorate the deepest and most central thing in them—their whole conscious, personal being." (*EGT*) Paul's prayer in other words is that God's Spirit may work mightily in believers; that each one may be filled with the (power of) the Spirit. "Be filled with the Spirit" (5:18)— and strengthened with the power of the Spirit (cf. Col 1:11).

2. That Christ may dwell in your hearts through faith —

That Christ may dwell—*katoikzoai*—another *oikos* word. The church, corporately and personally, is "a dwelling place of God in the Spirit" (*oikodomz*) (2:22 RSV). We find here again the idea of God's dwelling, inhabiting, tabernaculing among his people.[18] An interesting and fruitful study here would be to compare the two Greek verbs *oikew*, "to inhabit" (and cognates) and *okzvow*, "to dwell (in a tent)." The former word is rooted in Greek language and culture while the latter recalls Hebrew history and the Old Testament tabernacle. In general, Paul seems to prefer *oikew* (Rom 7:17-20; 1 Cor 3:16, etc.) while John often uses *okmvow* for essentially the same idea (Jn 1:14; Rev 7:15, 21:3, etc.; see the *Theological Dictionary of the New Testament*).

We have been made alive through faith in Jesus Christ, and now he dwells in the hearts of believers and in the Christian community. Paul's prayer implies not only a *continuing* of this dwelling, but a *deepening* of its reality and significance. "Through faith" implies a living relationship. We have been saved "by grace, through faith." Through this fact and act of salvation Jesus entered our life. But the relationship of faith continues and deepens. Jesus not only *saves*;

---

[18] See "Churches, Temples, and Tabernacles," Chapter 4 in Snyder, *Problem of Wineskins*.

he *indwells* in a relationship maintained by faith and obedience.

These first two requests of Paul are related in several ways. Both speak of the essential spiritual nature of the person—the "inner man," the "heart." Both imply the inhabiting presence of God—being filled with the Spirit or being indwelt by Jesus Christ have the same meaning. As Jesus the Spirit dwells in our hearts through faith we are strengthened with might in our innermost being. (Paul writes in Philippians 1:19, "I know that through your prayers and the help of the Spirit of Jesus Christ this will turn out for my deliverance.")

Throughout these passages we should keep reminding ourselves that Paul constantly uses "you" in the plural form. This of course includes personal or "individual" experience. But Paul is especially addressing the believing community, the community of Jesus' disciples. Everything he says has a doubly relational sense: Relationship first with God, but also mutually with one another. We must guard against the individualizing tendency, particularly in the West, which so focuses on each person's own spiritual experience that it misses the primarily corporate, shared identity we have in Christ in his body.

3. That you may be rooted and grounded in love —

Much could be said here, but for our purposes it is sufficient to call attention in this phrase to the emphasis on *love*, a word repeated some 20 times in Ephesians.

Here again the idea is related to the spiritual growth and maturity of the inner person. Paul prays that the Ephesian Christians may be strengthened with power, rooted and grounded in love, through the habitation through faith of the Holy Spirit in their lives and in their community.

These first three petitions in Paul's prayer call attention to the *essential spiritual nature* of human beings. Paul prays that we may be deeply, permanently, and dynamically converted to Jesus Christ. He wants believers at the center of their being to be truly Christian. This can come only through the miracle of Jesus Christ the Spirit dwelling in our hearts, in our Christian community, through faith.

Here we have already a partial answer to the question as to *how* the church can and should fulfill God's cosmic plan for the church. The answer *begins* with this: Be genuinely converted! Be totally Christian! Be fully the body of Christ. Be deeply indwelt by the power and love of Jesus Christ. At the very center of your being, be conformed to the nature of Jesus. It is at this point, and *only* at this point, that the church can and must begin the realization of God's cosmic plan.

Paul's language and use of organic metaphors suggests of course that this is not a once-for-all event. He expects the Ephesian Christians to grow in grace (as he emphasizes in chapter four). He urges Christians to be more and more truly Christian; to grow in grace and in the Spirit.

3:18 — *That you may have power to comprehend . . . what is the breadth and length and height and depth —*

"Power to comprehend" here refers to the capacity to understand—that you may be able fully to understand. "The breadth and length and height and depth"—of what? What is it concerning which we should have this comprehension? Undoubtedly it is related to the love of Christ (vs 19). And yet in light of the larger context and Paul's elaboration of the cosmic plan of God and of the phrase "power to comprehend," we may well wonder whether Paul is not thinking more largely here. It is as though Paul is saying, "May God grant you the capacity to grasp all this that I am saying here!" He speaks of a comprehension beyond the merely rational, but growing to the profoundly spiritual to the fullest capacities! May you grow in love, and may you also grow in your understanding of God's marvelous plan, shown through the unsearchable love of Christ! May you have an increasing comprehension of all that God wishes to do through the church and *through you* as persons and the believing community.

3:19 — *[That you may] know the love of Christ that surpasses knowledge* —

"The love of Christ that surpasses knowledge" indicates the sublimity and infinity of Christ's love. There is no measuring or exhaustively understanding this love of Christ. It can never be fully comprehended by finite minds. It is impossible fully to comprehend "the breadth and length and height and depth" of this love. But we can experience it! We can know it by experience, personal knowledge. The more we experience it, the more we see that it "surpasses knowledge."

Paul's concern here is for the personal experiencing of the love of Christ—again, Christ's dwelling in the heart and in the community; the inner strengthening of the Holy Spirit.

3:19 — *That you may be filled with all the fullness of God* —

In rigidly logical (or physical) categories, this statement would make no sense at all! Yet it makes profound perfect sense—the fullness of God's presence through the habitation of Jesus Christ the Spirit. This petition summarizes the previous ones and says more fully what God wants for the church and each believer: "that you may be filled with all the fulness of God." "Be filled with the Spirit" (5:18).

What then is the cumulative force of these various petitions? What is the significance for Paul's overall theme of God's cosmic plan through the church?

Essentially, Paul's petitions boil down to two: You the church, be powerfully indwelt by the Spirit of Christ and grow in your comprehension of God's will, God's plan.

As these two petitions are answered, the church already begins to make known to the principalities and powers the manifold wisdom of God. Of course there is much more to the fulfillment of God's cosmic plan, as we shall see. But as the church grows in the knowledge and experience of God and his purposes, it *does* begin to fulfill God's overall design.

3:20 — *Now to him who by the power at work within us is able to accomplish abundantly far more than all that we ask or imagine* —

Paul reminds readers of God's greatness and power. Have no small vision of what God can do through the church! He is well able to do far more than we have asked, far more than we have ever imagined. God is abundantly able to carry out his cosmic plan, fantastic as it may seem to the human mind. This is the Scripture promise: and this, "by the power [of the Holy Spirit] *at work within us*." Paul is emphasizing what God is capable of doing through the church. Incredible as it may seem, God is able to accomplish his cosmic plan through the church. What a challenge to our faith!

3:21 — *To him be glory in the church and in Christ Jesus to all generations, for ever and ever. Amen.* —

This is a central *purpose* of all God's plan—"to him be glory in the church." The realization of God's design, and its realization through the church, is in order that God may be glorified. All glory be to God in the church! "And in Christ Jesus," the head of the church, shows that head and body are now inseparable. Jesus is joined to the church as he dwells among and within the believers by the Spirit. "To all generations, for ever and ever": once again the cosmic dimension. God's plan and the glory he receives continue to the end of human history and well beyond. "Amen." On this sublime note Paul closes his prayer, and with it the first half of the epistle. What remains now is to work out more specifically what God's plan means for each member of the church, and for the church's corporate life.

Chapter 4

An Earthly Body for Christ

Paul now gives in chapter four his most profound and succinct teaching about what the church *is* and how it is to *function* as a living spiritual-social-physical organism.

4:1 — Lead a life worthy of the calling to which you have been called —

You, the church: having been saved by faith, Christ the Spirit working powerfully in the very center of your being, *lead the life* of true Christians. It is to this emphasis on the daily walk that Paul now turns. This theme was already foreshadowed in 2:10: "For we are his workmanship, created in Christ Jesus for good works, which God prepared beforehand, that we should walk in them" (RSV). Both passages refer to God's overall purpose: works "prepared beforehand" and a life "worthy of the calling to which you have been called."

Paul in his writings repeatedly makes this same emphasis on the importance of the Christian's daily walk—for example in Phil 1:27, Col 1:10, and 1 Thess 2:12.

What does a life truly worthy of the calling we have received actually look like?

4:2 — with all humility and gentleness, with patience, bearing with one another in love —

Paul has in view the attitudes and behaviors, the "mind" and worldview and mission of true followers of Christ, especially in relation to other members of Jesus' body.

"Humility"—a clear estimate of ourselves in the light of God's revelation and in light of our co-membership in Christian community. In other words, not thinking of oneself more highly than one ought to think. An attitude that springs from true love. "Gentleness" or "meekness"— This biblical word emphatically does *not* mean a "doormat complex," the idea that one is of no value and is simply to let oneself to be used by any and everyone. It is a word of strength, not of weakness—consider the meekness of Moses! It signifies a life that is so strongly and confidently grounded in God that we have the inner strength to seek, not our own will, by the will of God and the good of others. With this basis, thus rooted in a confident relationship with God, we are to relate to others with gentleness. But there is another side: a holy boldness to speak out for God and righteousness and rebuke, in no uncertain terms, the powers of evil.

"Patience" (or "long-suffering," KJV), not in relation to evil, but in relation to the trials and problems we have to endure at times. Patience is one of the most needed of Christian virtues, and one clearly demonstrated in God's dealings with humans. Biblical history shows JHWH to be the patient God. Think of the patience of Jesus Christ. Jesus, sometimes "troubled in spirit" (Jn 13:21) though generally calm, unperturbed, unhurried, though agonizing for us, for the church, for the world's redemption, the restoration of creation.

"Bearing with one another in love"—a key calling, quality, and behavior of the *koinonia* of God's people, the fellowship of the body of Christ. Forbearing one another in love is no mere enduring, passively and withdrawn, the weaknesses of others. It is a sharing, a "consoling," a comforting, one of the other, within the Christian community. It is the "bearing of one another's burdens" which makes the Christian *koinonia* healing, helpful, strengthening.

4:3 — *Making every effort to maintain the unity of the Spirit in the bond of peace* —

The "unity of the Spirit" is the unity which the Spirit gives or produces and a reflection of the Trinity. Here begins Paul's emphasis on oneness and unity within the community of believers. This fits in precisely, however, with what he has already said about God's eternal plan "to unite all things in him" (1:10; cf. 2:14ff).

Where the Spirit works, he produces unity. But this is not the unity of uniformity. Rather it is the unity of diversity—the same unity in diversity seen gloriously in all God's creation and about which Paul will shortly speak.

But we must be "eager to maintain" (RSV) or "make every effort to maintain" this unity within the church. To a large extent the working and preservation of this unity depends on us. This is part of our "foreordained good works." This also is part of God's plan for us whereby Jesus through the church makes known his manifold wisdom.

We pause here to consider in more detail the relevance of these first three verses of chapter four in relation to God's eternal plan through the church.

Note first the transition in emphasis from the end of chapter three to the beginning of chapter four. Having declared what is

God's eternal purpose "through the church," Paul in 3:14–19 shows that the fulfillment of this purpose begins with Christians first of all *being* something. Having been made alive (2:1, 5), they are to be inhabited by the strengthening, dynamic, transforming Spirit of our Lord Jesus Christ, growing both in love and in the comprehension of God's will.

Now in chapter four Paul moves from an emphasis on *being* to an emphasis on *doing* or acting— "Lead a life"—lead the life of a Christian. Paul now emphasizes the Christian walk. Not in an isolated or exclusively "individual" sense, though, for Paul consistently stresses the Christian community, the life of the church. In fact, 4:1–3 focuses primarily on relationships within the church.

This suggests that when believers realize and participate in a community (that is, the church, the body of Christ,) marked by love, unity, peace and the other virtues mentioned here, they are on their way to fulfilling God's eternal plan. That plan is already being fulfilled in part when the church truly exists as the communion or fellowship (*koinonia*) of the Holy Spirit (2 Cor 13:13).[19]

Paul here shows us the first two steps in the fulfillment of God's eternal plan through the church. 1) Be at the center of your being truly Christian through the Spirit's indwelling; 2) demonstrate the reality of the Christian community among yourselves, in the church. Or, using the language of reconciliation and going back to include the earlier step of being "saved by faith" and "made alive," we may put it this way: 1) Be (each of you) reconciled to God. 2) Be indwelt

---

[19] See Chapter 7, "The Fellowship of the Holy Spirit," in Snyder, *Problem of Wineskins.*

by God (a continuing, deeper, inward reconciliation). 3) Be reconciled each to the other within the community (that is, the church); demonstrate the reconciled life among yourselves.

This is an oversimplification, but it does suggest a certain progression revealed here in Ephesians concerning God's eternal plan through the church. God is working *now* and through history through the church to fulfill his plan. We are and are called to be part of it!

4:4 — There is one body and one Spirit, just as you were called to the one hope of your calling —

This statement gives "the objective ground, or basis in fact, on which the walk in lowliness, meekness, longsuffering and loving forbearance is urged, and of which it should be the result" (*EGT*). The "unity of the Spirit" should and must be maintained because in fact there is but one Spirit and one God and one faith. Therefore there can be but one body and one hope.

"One body" — Clearly, the body of Christ, the united community of believers (cf. 1:22-23, 2:16, 3:6, etc.). This is an objective fact: there is but one body. It is now a given reality. But the problem of reconciling this with "the sociological fact of the church" is real enough.

"One hope" — The way of Christ remains the way of hope. Those without Christ were without hope in the world (2:12). But now we have hope—not based on mere longing, but based on what God has *done* and what he has *promised*. It is a hope well-anchored (Heb 6:17-20)—a hope not just of personal salvation, but of the reconciliation of all things; creation healed; the Kingdom of God in fullness.

4:5 — One Lord, one faith, one baptism —

Paul is deeply impressed with the overall unity and oneness of God's plan. Since this plan is to reconcile "all things" in Christ, "things in heaven and things on earth" (1:10), the fact of one Lord, faith, and baptism naturally follows. This unity Paul emphasizes here is the result of the fact of the oneness of the Triune God and the unity of his plan for the created universe.

"One Lord" evidently refers to Jesus Christ, considering verses 4 and 6. The "one faith" refers first of all to saving faith (i.e., "one means of access to God through faith in Jesus Christ") but also has the more general sense of the faith Christians now share as a body of convictions and confessions about Jesus' incarnation, life, death, resurrection, and ongoing reign leading to the coming of the kingdom of God in fullness, interpreted as fulfillment of Old Testament promises. This latter sense is evident in Paul's writings elsewhere. For example, 1 Timothy 4:6, "If you put these instructions before the brothers and sisters, you will be a good servant of Christ Jesus, nourished on the words of the faith and of the sound teaching that you have followed." Or similarly Galatians 1:23, ". . . they only heard it said, 'The one who formerly was persecuting us is now proclaiming the faith he once tried to destroy.'"

The whole sweep of Paul's writings here makes it clear that the phrase "one faith" definitely should *not* be understood as mere intellectual assent to a creed or set of doctrines—a concept foreign to the gospel and vital discipleship.

4:6 — One God and Father of all, who is above all and through all and in all —

Here the fact of unity reaches its culmination. There is, finally, one body, one Spirit, one faith, because God is One, and there is but one God and Father of us all. Here Paul's thinking returns to its cosmic dimension because God is in fact "above all and through all and in all." This, obviously, not in any pantheistic sense, as the context makes clear enough. This statement includes but greatly transcends what truth there is in pantheism. It points to both transcendence and immanence, both the ultimacy and intimacy of the Triune God.

But how can God be "Father of us all" when not all believe in him or in Jesus Christ? It is in Jesus Christ that we become sons and daughters of God. The context could suggest that Paul is speaking here only of believers—"us all" meaning everyone within the community of faith. The context is the church. God fills and indwells, but also "overflows," the church, for he is also "above all and through all and in all." Thus the sphere and activity of Christians' lives is not limited (narrowly understood) to the church. We are *now* "in the heavenly places," in that overlapping reality of the material spacetime world and the mostly unseen spirit world. Biblically speaking, the whole material world exists of course wholly within the much vaster, infinite world of God's existence and God's reign. There is no cosmic dualism here.

Here we should refer back to Ephesians 3:15, where Paul writes that from the Father "every family [or "all fatherhood"] in heaven and on earth takes its name." Paul keeps reminding us and himself of God's transcendence and sovereignty. The Lord God is the source of all human being—and thus the "Father" of all human families, not just of Christians. There is truth in the phrase, "The Fatherhood of God and the brotherhood of man"—that is, the kinship of all human

87

beings everywhere through history because God is Creator and Sustainer. God is in fact Father of the whole human race. But it is only through Jesus Christ, Head and body, that humans come to experience the humanness that God intends, the shared life, the community and meaning, and the vocation which gospel living in the body of Christ makes possible and real.

Christians should keep in mind this double sense of fatherhood (or parenthood) and family. As Christians, we are uniquely, experientially sisters and brothers in the body of Christ. But every person everywhere is our brother or sister in our shared humanity and thus in our shared concern and responsibility—both our Christian responsibility and the human responsibility we share with everyone everywhere due to creation and God's everlasting covenant with the earth (Gen 9:8-17).[20]

These three verses—Ephesians 4:4-6—emphatically stress the unity of the faith. Paul no doubt has in mind the divisions and factionalism that had entered into some local churches. This emphasis on unity was necessary.

This focus on unity also makes sense in the context of Paul's basic theme of God's cosmic plan for the church, as we have noted. Paul's language implies that through its *unity* and *oneness* the church also bears witness to, and fulfills, God's eternal plan for the church. A part of the way God works through the church to reconcile all things is by the reconciliation he brings *within* the church; the unity demonstrated within and among believers.

We note however here that unity is not the only—and not

---

[20] See God's earth covenant in *Salvation Means Creation Healed*, especially Chapter 8.

necessarily the most important —way in which God fulfills his cosmic plan. This must be said in the face of any form of ecumenicity that would make visible unity *the* test of and basis for the fulfillment of God's plan. If there is not first the fact of "being made alive," if Christ does not "dwell in your hearts through faith," if there is not the love of Christ, then oneness loses its basis and therefore its significance. Certainly there is, legitimately, a large area here for concern and action so that spiritual unity in Christ may be manifest visibly. But ultimately this has meaning only as there is the prior basis of personal reconciliation and the deep working of God within the community of believers.

4:7 — *But each of us was given grace according to the measure of Christ's gift —*

But grace is given to each one! We have a key transition now. There is one God and Spirit, one faith and baptism, "but"! This unity does not preclude diversity. It is not uniformity. We are one, *but*. But what? But God is working in each person, according to his or her capacity and according to God's gift. *But grace*. The grace of God shows itself in multifold ways within the Christian community, as light through a prism. As we are saved by grace, so we exercise the gifts of the Spirit by grace (See 1 Pt 4:10-11).

"Naturally there are different gifts and functions; individually grace is given to us in different ways out of the rich diversity of Christ's giving" (Phillips paraphrase). God's supreme gift to us is the gift of his grace through Christ, seen preeminently in the salvation that we receive through faith. But this grace is given "to each of us" according to our necessity and according to God's will for each one in the light of each person's capacities and talents (which already are a gift). The one gift of grace *refracts* itself into varied and various manifestations, so that each person is capacitated to fulfill their place in the community for the edification of the whole and the fulfillment of the mission of the church in the world. Here begins the diversity within the unity.

4:8 — *Therefore it is said, "When he ascended on high he made captivity itself a captive; he gave gifts to his people"* —

A reference to Psalm 68:18, but not a direct quote (either from the Hebrew or the LXX). The older RSV translation perhaps reflects better the Old Testament source: "He led a host of captives, and gave gifts to men." Psalm 68:18 however speaks of "receiving gifts," not giving them. Paul apparently was following accepted Rabbinic interpretation of the passage, but applying it to Christ. (See exegesis in *The Interpreter's Bible*). This also reflects what might be called the gospel reversal: Old Testament kings (even Hebrew ones) received gifts *from* their captives, but Jesus graciously takes captivity itself captive and *gives* gifts—preeminently the give of himself and of God's grace, and the gift of the body of Christ itself.

Among the Jews this passage was commonly interpreted as referring to Moses ascending Mt. Sinai and there receiving the law. Paul's point is simply that Jesus Christ, in "ascending on high," distributed the gift of his grace to each believer in such a way that we can speak of his "gifts" (plural). The operation of the various gifts in the church is the result of Christ's giving.

4:9 — *When it says, "He ascended," what does it mean but that he had also descended into the lower parts of the earth?—*

Paul likely has in mind Christ's "descent," in the twofold sense of Jesus' incarnation (cf. Phil 2:5-10). The point Paul is making gains its significance especially from the following verse: it is the cosmic Christ of whom he is speaking. This Christ who gives gifts to men and women is the same who came down from heaven, was dead, buried, but rose again to "fill all things."

4:10 — *He who descended is the same one who also ascended far above all the heavens, that he might fill all things* —

In "descending" and "ascending," Jesus Christ tasted and experienced "all things." Nothing is outside the knowledge of Christ. His ascension is so "that he might fill all things"—an echo of the cosmic theme of this whole letter.

4:11 — *The gifts he gave were that some should be apostles, some prophets, some evangelists, some pastors and teachers* —

The most important related New Testament passages here are Romans 12:6-8 and 1 Corinthians 12:8-10, 28. Here in Ephesians and in these other passages we find four different listings by Paul of the Spirit's gifts. Although the lists are essentially similar, Paul has a somewhat different point in mind, in terms of the functioning of the gifts, in 1 Corinthians 12:28 and Ephesians 4:11 than he does in Romans 12:6-8 and 1 Corinthians 12:8-10.

In Romans, Paul is concerned to show that "we, who are many, are one body in Christ, and individually we are members one of another" (12:5). The emphasis is on the diversity within the unity in the body of Christ.

The concern is essentially the same in 1 Cor. 12:8-10 in that "there are varieties of activities, but it is the same God who activates all of them in everyone. To each is given the manifestation of the Spirit for the common good" (12:6-7).

Thus in both these two instances, the emphasis is on *the fact of the gifts themselves*. Paul speaks of prophecy, teaching, healing, etc., not of prophets, teachers, healers, etc.

But Paul has something else in mind here in Ephesians 4:11 and in 1 Cor. 12:28. His emphasis or preoccupation is clear in the latter passage: "and God has appointed in the church . . . ." The emphasis is not on the gifts in themselves, but on the order of the church; the way God has provided for the proper functioning of the gifts within the body. Paul is saying, in effect, in this entire chapter: There are the gifts of the Spirit: utterance of wisdom, faith, healing, prophecy, for example. Now, this is the way God provides for the functioning of the church in the light of these gifts: He has appointed in the church his apostles, prophets, teachers, administrators, and so forth. We see clearly further on in 1 Corinthians how Paul's basic concern is the edification of the church (14:3-5, 12, 26).

Thus the passage here in Ephesians 4:11 is directly parallel to 1 Corinthians 12:28, and only secondarily to 1 Corinthians 12:8-10 and Romans 12:6-8. Paul here shows the various functions to be exercises within the church (apostles, prophets, evangelists, pastors and teachers), and states clearly the purpose of these functions: "to equip the saints for the work of ministry" (Eph 4:12).

Paul is obviously not referring here to an organizational or structured hierarchy. He is showing that God himself has provided for order within the church by providing within each local congregation those capable of exercising the various necessary functions. The principles behind this order are relational, organic, and ecological in the sense of mutual interrelationship.

It is clear also, given the difference between Ephesians 4:11 and 1 Corinthians 12:28 and given the whole tenor of the New Testament, that there was (as yet) no fixed list of functions or offices in the church. God provides within each local congregation the leaders necessary, and this may very well vary from congregation to congregation. Therefore it is unnecessary—and probably unwise—to think in terms of a fixed number or order of leaders, the same for each church. Not all local churches need, or should have, the same structure of leadership. God will give, through his Spirit, to each what is needed.

This, then, is the first important fact we should note here: God has not given to the church a hierarchical structure of leadership, or even the same number or kind of leaders for all local churches. Rather, he provides within each branch of the church those leaders necessary to its proper functioning and edification.[21]

In the light of this, there is no crucial significance in the difference between these two lists of gifts (1 Cor 12:28 and Eph 4:11). In 1 Corinthians, Paul is still thinking about the fact of diversity, and so he lists *all* the varied basic functions within the church. In Ephesians, however, Paul is showing how the various gifts work together within the church; *how* they function. Common to the two lists are apostles, prophets, and teachers. In Ephesians evangelists and pastors join the list, which may be considered the further subdividing of those Paul was including in 1 Corinthians as apostles, prophets, and teachers. These five, then, we may consider as the basic leadership functions which God the Spirit provides within the church: apostles, prophets, evangelists, pastors, and

---

[21] I develop this further in my book *Community of the King*.

teachers.

In the last few decades it has become a popular error in some circles to make *too much* of this so-called "fivefold ministry." We must always be conscious that this is a description of a dynamic, organic, ecological pattern of leadership in the church. The functions themselves are the important point, not the terminology. These are not "offices," and the functions need not be wedded to these specific linguistic terms, since language is dynamic. Particular terms can mean one thing in one time and context but come to have quite another in another time and context. Consider the very different ways the terms "bishop" and "pastor" are understood in different church and cultural contexts, for example.

In 1 Corinthians 12:28, after mentioning "*first* apostles, *second* prophets, *third* teachers," Paul mentions several other functions: "*then* workers of miracles" and an array of other gifts. A natural division seems implied here, as though Paul were saying, "God has appointed in the church, first of all, apostles, prophets, and teachers. Beyond these there are the more particular or limited gifts of healing, helping, and so forth." There is thus a seeming parallel between these two passages, as follow:

Ephesians 4:11		1 Corinthians 12:28
Apostles, prophets, evangelists, pastors, teachers	← →	Apostles, prophets, teachers
For the equipment of the saints for the work of the ministry	← →	Workers of miracles, healers, helpers, administrators, tongues-speakers

In other words, apostles, prophets, evangelists, pastors and teachers are given *to* the church to exercise an equipping ministry, preparing each member for *his or her* work of ministry. And what is this work of ministry? For each member it may be different, but we see some of the things it involves: healing, helping, administering, and so forth in a somewhat fluid pattern of charisms. In all cases the final goal is the same: "so that the church may be built up" or "edified" (1 Cor 14:5); so that "all of us come to the unity of the faith and of the knowledge of the Son of God, to maturity, to the measure of the full stature of Christ" (Eph 4:13).

Note especially here that these leaders (apostles, prophets, evangelists, pastors, teachers) are *God's gift,* not primarily *the church's choice* or the choice of its officials. These gifted leaders "God has appointed in the church" (1 Cor 12:28); they are his "gifts" to the church (Eph 4:11). This means it is the task of the church to *discover,* to discern by the Spirit, which persons God is calling to these functions. It is God who calls and chooses, not human beings. It is the church which, through prayer, discussion, observation, and waiting on God, seeks to learn from God himself which persons are called to each function.

This obviously implies a high degree of flexibility—more than exists in the average institutional church. In highly structured or organized churches the method is, first, to decide what functions (offices, officers, chairpersons, teachers, etc.) are necessary, then to seek people to fit each slot. This is an inversion of the biblical direction. The church should start with *people.* Who are the leaders God is giving to the church? What are their gifts of leadership? What fruit is emerging? Then, in prayer, each person is given responsibility according to their gift.

If "there are not enough qualified leaders to go around" (a frequent complaint), this is good sign that 1) we have an unbiblical concept of leadership; 2) we have more "officers," "superintendents," "chairpersons," or whatever, than are really necessary; and 3) we are trying to fill out an organizational chart rather than help each person find their God-given ministry. For God's Word is clear enough here: *He will give to his church the leaders that are really necessary.* If it seems that God is not doing this, it is because we have misunderstood the biblical nature of the church and the true significance of the Spirit's gifts.

What functions are really necessary in the church? Paul summarizes these as apostles, prophets, evangelists, pastors and teachers. These are God's leadership gifts *to* the church to equip the church for its work of ministry—a key point, rich both theologically and practically.

We must enquire briefly into the meaning of these specific kinds of leaders. There has been much discussion as to the meaning of these various functions in the context of the early church, and many attempts to find out just how they were understood in the time of Paul and immediately afterwards. William Barclay suggested this:

> In the early church these were three kinds of office-bearers. There were a few whose writ and whose authority ran throughout the whole church [i.e., the apostles]. There were many whose ministry was not confined to one place, but who carried out a wandering ministry, going wherever the Spirit moved them, and where God sent them [prophets and evangelists]. There were some whose ministry was a local ministry which was confined to the one congregation and to the one place [i.e., pastors and teachers].[22]

---

[22] William Barclay, *The Letters to the Galatians and Ephesians* (Edinburgh: Saint Andrews Press, 1966), 171.

This is helpful and essentially correct. However the term "office-bearers" is misleading, as it implies a concept of "office" (an organizational position to be filled) that developed after the New Testament age and is not found in the New Testament. Paul's focus is on people and function, not on official position or status.

Paul is reflecting here on the various leaders who had already emerged in the church. But it would be misleading to take Paul's words here merely as a description of existing leadership patterns, and even less as a divine baptism on such patterns as had already appeared. This has been the tendency however of much commentary on this passage—to see the passage simply as showing what forms of leadership had already appeared. See for example Eduard Schweizer, *Church Order in the New Testament*.[23]

More than mere description, this Ephesian passage is also *revelation*. Through Paul, God's Spirit here reveals *God's* order for the proper functioning of the body of Christ. Obviously there were "apostles, prophets, evangelists, pastors, and teachers" in the early church. The question—still highly relevant today—is, how did these leaders actually function, and what do these general types of leadership functions teach us today?

This perspective on Paul's intention makes a big difference in the way we interpret the various functions Paul mentions. It is crucial in asking about apostles, for instance, whether these persons exercised a particular, specific leadership function which passed away when the original apostles (the eyewitnesses of the resurrection) died, or whether God intends apostolic leadership to

---

[23] Eduard Schweizer, *Church Order in the New Testament* (London: SCM Press, 1961), 194ff.

continue in the church today—another point that has been widely discussed throughout history and in recent decades.

With these considerations in mind, we may consider briefly each of the function specifically mentioned here in 4:11.

Apostles— Paul was highly conscious of himself being an apostle, and of the apostolic ministry in general. The church is "built upon the foundation of the apostles and prophets, Christ Jesus himself being the chief cornerstone" (Eph 2:20). God's plan through the church "has now been revealed to his holy apostles and prophets by the Spirit" (3:5).

In the early church, an apostle apparently was one recognized as having a place of preeminent leadership and authority throughout the entire church. The original apostles—that is, the 11 disciples of Jesus, plus Paul—were recognized as having particular authority because of their nearness to Christ. They had seen him and been witnesses of his resurrection, although in the case of Paul this was by visions and direct revelation.

But others in the early church were also considered to be apostles: Barnabas, Silas, and probably also James, Andronicus, and Junia (Acts 14:4, 14; 1 Cor 15:7; Gal 1:9; 1 Thess 2:6; Rom 16:7). So it cannot really be argued that the apostolic ministry passed away with the death of the original 12. Indeed, Paul's words here show just the opposite: the Spirit gives the function of apostle to the church as he chooses.

A whole ecclesiastical mythology has grown up around the function of apostolic ministry in the church: ideas of "apostolic succession" (rigidly interpreted), and so forth. But what we have here is simply 1) general leaders for the church 2) whose place and authority are recognized throughout the church 3) because it is recognized that God's Spirit has raised them up. They are general leaders whose authority is based in the fact of their being raised up by God and in their faithfulness to revealed truth—that is, the Bible and the life, teachings, and resurrection of Jesus. Their authority is contingent upon their faithfulness as witnesses. Ceasing to witness faithfully to the truth of God's revelation, they cease to have authority.

Apostles, then, for today are the church's general leaders, those who have responsibility for the general oversight of the church. These are the leaders God chooses as witnesses to his revelation and guardians of that revelation.

How do the truly divinely-appointed apostles come to be recognized and to exercise their role? This raises the question of organizational structure, which the New Testament does not discuss. Presumably a variety of organizational patters are possible. Probably it makes little difference, biblically, whether these apostles are called bishops, superintendents, moderators, presidents, or whatever. The important things are that 1) the structure be sufficiently flexible and open so that the "apostles" can truly exercise their New Testament function (admittedly a rare thing in most churches), and similarly, that 2) the means of appointing these leaders be such that there is a sensitivity to the voice of the Holy Spirit so that those humanly chosen are indeed the ones God is choosing.

The question arises here as to the relationship, in Paul's thinking, between apostles and bishops (1 Tim 4:1ff, Tit 1:5ff). This question will be treated a little later.

It should be obvious that there is no authority *inherent* in the "office" of apostle — simply because the apostolate is not, in itself, an *office* to be given to a person chosen by the church. Apostleship is a *function* exercised by apostles. God has not established in the church *the offices of* apostle, prophet, evangelist, pastor, and teacher. This would be to think in static, institutional terms. Rather, "his gifts were that some should be apostles, some prophets," etc. The gift from God is *persons*, not *offices*. This distinction is crucial, especially today because of our tendency to think in institutional and organizational, rather than personal and charismatic (and thus biblical), terms.

This means that whatever authority an apostle exercises is based on what he or she is as a person through whom God works, not on the office they hold. It is by grace *intrinsic*, not *extrinsic*, authority.

This raises again questions of organizational structure, to be further discussed later.

Prophets — Note that Paul twice links prophets with apostles in Ephesians. We know something of the function of prophets in the primitive church. According to Barclay, "The prophets were wanderers throughout the Church. Their message was held to be not the result of thought and study, but the direct result of the Holy Spirit. They had no homes and no families and no means of support. They went from Church to Church proclaiming the will of God as God had told it to them."[24] It is obvious by Paul's usage here that the prophets, like apostles, were recognized as having a general and preeminent ministry through the church. In a somewhat different sense, prophecy was a gift often exercised by particular persons within the local church (cf. 1 Cor 14:26-40).

---

[24] William Barclay, *The Letters to the Galatians and Ephesians* (Edinburgh: Saint Andrews Press, 1966), 172.

Translating the prophetic function to the present day, who are the prophets, if not the so-called "charismatic leaders" that spring up in the church? (I use the term "charismatic" here not in the sense of *glossolalia* but in the more general sense of persons who emerge, without any official leadership position, as generally recognized spiritual leaders.) Almost every denomination has in its history those men and women who have risen up—or whom the Spirit has raised up—and whom all recognize as leaders and persons of God, even though they may have no official church office. Many times such women and men become the traveling evangelists and special speakers in the church. Or, they may raise up special organizations or movements within or parallel to the organized church—youth movements, missionary organizations, and so forth. Or they may eventually be tapped for denominational leadership—bishop or general officer.

Many times however charismatic leaders are passed over in choosing such official leaders because they are too independent and unpredictable for the office. Or, if actually chosen, they may refuse the office because they see it as too limiting. These persons, if truly anointed by God, are too big for the office previously created. (A good example of this is the missionary E. Stanley Jones in the Methodist Church.)

In other words, Ephesians makes provision here for particular "charismatic" leaders who emerge within the Christian community. If such persons are genuinely people of God, filled with the Spirit, they may be "prophets" whom God is raising up. Their ministries will be ministries of direct relationship to God. They will have all the power—and all the possibilities of being unconventional and unpredictable—of a true prophet. They will also be subject to the dangers of extremism, since their messages come directly from God, and their temptation will be to speak on their own and claim to be speaking for God. In these ways, we see a direct relationship to Old Testament prophets.

Prophets in the church may or may not be official leaders. This is incidental. They are constituted prophets by God's Holy Spirit, independent of any "official" position in the church. If the church is authentically spiritual, it will recognize the authenticity and immediacy of such prophetic ministry.

As in the Bible, so in the church: the prophet is God's instrument for speaking directly *to the church* (and perhaps, secondarily, to the world), speaking encouragement, exhortation, warning, or judgment, according to the situation. The validity of their message does not depend upon approval or acceptance by the church. Their message is valid only however if in harmony with the Bible. The Spirit of God is a Spirit of order, not confusion, and does not contradict himself.

So the church does not "choose" prophets. It only recognizes them and listens to them (or ignores them, to its peril). It may in one way or another sustain them. The appearance of true prophets in the church, we may be certain, is a sign of God's operation among his people, for he has promised to raise up his prophets.

Evangelists — A prophet may sometimes also be an evangelist, and vice versa.

The word "evangelist" does not occur often in the New Testament. This may seem surprising. The only other occurrences are Acts 21:8 ("Philip the evangelist") and 2 Timothy 4:5 ("do the work of an evangelist").

Why so few references? Does this mean the New Testament is

not especially concerned with evangelism? Hardly! Paul himself is eloquent proof to the contrary. But Paul—and the New Testament church in general—did not see evangelism as primarily the work of specialists—"evangelists." Evangelism simply happened. It was the natural expression and fruit of the life of the church. There was little need either to exhort the people to evangelism or to raise up a special class of evangelists. (See the discussion of the meaning of evangelism in *Salvation Means Creation Healed*, 141-44, and also Alan Kreider's fine book, *The Patient Ferment of the Early Church: The Improbable Rise of Christianity in the Roman Empire* [Baker, 2016].)

But if this is so, why then does Paul even mention evangelists at all in this passage? They are not mentioned in 1 Corinthians 12 or Romans 12.

The probable reason is the simple fact that Christians who were strictly evangelists, and recognized as such (in distinction to apostles and prophets, with whom they presumably had much in common) had arisen in the church, most notably, Philip. Paul recognized these as being within "God's ecclesiology." The growth of a healthy church does not depend on the work of "evangelists," for the church is a witnessing community. Yet a healthy church may properly have and profitably use such specially gifted persons. This was the situation in the early church.

Apostles were also evangelists, but Paul refers here to those whose function was limited more exclusively to evangelism and were not apostles. Particularly, in distinction from the apostles, the evangelists did not have responsibility for the general oversight of the church, though their function may have included the proclamation of the Good News *to* and *within* the Christian community as well as outside it. (See *TDNT*, 2:736-37). The primary function was always proclamation, "bearing the good news."

Thus, evangelist is a legitimate function in the church. We may expect God to raise up evangelists in our day, both within the local church and more generally. The church should be alert to recognize these people and should encourage and facilitate their work. The church should not, however, fall into the error of thinking that only such persons have responsibility for evangelism, as we shall see. And a healthy church, living in accord with Ephesians 4, will not make that mistake.

Pastors and teachers — These may be thought of as one group or two groups. Practically, it makes little difference. In any case, Paul here identifies two more or less distinct *functions*, the pastoral and the teaching ministries.

Here we are dealing for the most part with leaders on the local level, and more specifically those whose ministry is *to* and *within* the local congregation.

There is nothing here—or elsewhere in the New Testament—to suggest that "pastor" in the early church had anything like the highly specialized and professionalized sense it has come to have in contemporary Protestantism. In fact, this is the only time the word "pastors" occurs in the New Testament in the sense of congregational leaders, though the idea of the congregation as a flock to be cared for occurs in John 21:16; Acts 20:18; and 1 Peter 5:2.

We have here, then, not the pastoral *office* but simply the pastoral *function*. Among the functions necessary for the edification and growth of the church is that of pastor, shepherding. In a normal (that is, biblical) local congregation, God will raise up those (not just one) whose ministry is to shepherd the flock.

Part of this shepherding will be teaching. The teaching ministry was and is essential in the church. Paul elsewhere shows his concern for the teaching ministry (e.g. 1 Tim 3:2, 4:11-12; 2 Tim 2:2). He himself dedicated his time to teaching his converts in the cities he evangelized.

There is much to be taught. Doctrinal teaching, which is essential; teaching the disciplines of Christian living; training in various forms of witness; and Bible teaching in general. Whatever else may be taught in the local church, this surely must be the "core curriculum."

These then are the four "equipping ministries" of which Paul speaks—apostles, prophets, evangelists, and pastor-teachers. They are God's gift to the church "to equip the saints for the work of ministry."

Each present-day denomination, and each local church, should sit down with this list and also with a list of its current organizational structure and, before God, compare them. How does the church actually function—compared with what the Word says here? *Is the practical application of Ephesians 4:11–16 even possible in our church given its present structure?* If not, what would God have us do? In some cases, the choice may actually be between throwing out our present organizational structure—or throwing out the Bible.

4:12 — *to equip the saints for the work of ministry for building up the body of Christ* —

Here we have the *purpose* of the various functions mentioned in 4:11. I have purposely left out the comma (or commas) usually inserted in this verse. What the Word says here is much clearer without them. Adding commas after "saints" or "ministry," as some versions do, gives a twist to the passage that is not contained or intended in the original. God has given these leaders to the church precisely to prepare and equip the saints for *their* work of ministry so that the body of Christ may be edified. (cf. *EGT*: "Christ gave some men as apostles, some as prophets, etc., with a view to the full equipment of the saints for the work of ministration of service they have each to do in order to the building up of the body of Christ! The building up of the Church—that is the great aim and final object, to that every believer has his contribution to make; and to qualify all for this is the purpose of Christ in giving 'Apostles, prophets, evangelists, pastors and teachers'" [3:331].

This means, among other things, that the chief ministry of pastors and teachers is *to the church*—not in the sense of mere counsel and comfort, of "holding the hands of the saints," but in the sense of *equipping, training, preparing* all members for *their* "work of ministry," preparing them spiritually and practically.

We commonly have two mistaken models of the church in this respect. One may be pictured as follows:

Church → Leaders (Pastors, Teachers) → World

According to this understanding, the function of church leaders is to do the work of ministry in the world. The leaders are those chosen by the church to carry on the church's ministry in the world. According to Ephesians 4:11-12, this concept is obviously wrong.

The second misleading model can be pictured this way:

Church → Leaders → Church

The idea here is that the leaders, coming from or chosen by the church, have a ministry primarily (or exclusively) *to* the church.

Their function is to "edify" the church, but this is understood in a superficial and introverted sense—not of *equipping* the saints, but merely of serving them, waiting on them, as one might care for a bed-ridden invalid. This is what I call "holding the hands of the saints." When the saints are, literally and physically, bed-ridden invalids, this kind of ministry has some merit. But when the members are *spiritually* invalid, a different kind of ministry is needed. They need to be told, and helped, to get up and walk.

What is the biblical pattern, according to Ephesians? Basically this:

Leaders   →   Church   →   World

Here the function of God-inspired leaders is to prepare the church for *her* work of ministry—both to the world and to the church itself. The ministry of these leaders is indeed to the church, but not as an end in itself. It doesn't end there. Pastoral ministry is successful *only* if the saints are equipped for *and actually do* their work of ministry. And this work will have its direction both toward the church and toward the world.

We may analyze further these two verses as follows:

Apostles, prophets, etc. → equipping saints → ministry → building Christ's Body

The key outcome of the saints' work of ministry is *the building up of the body of Christ.*

It is interesting here (as we will discuss more fully later) that this leadership plan is seen in terms of *edifying the church*, not in terms of the salvation of the lost, of evangelism. But remember Paul's basic theme: God's eternal plan through the church. God's plan or economy is to reconcile all things; to unite all things in Christ through the church. This plan has its cosmic dimensions—

but still it is *through the church*. The church is more than just an instrument or tool. It is an entity, a being in itself, and of supreme value to God. It is the body of Christ; more, it is the bride of Christ. This figure implies not only the holiness and purity God desires of the church, but its *supreme value* in God's eyes.

So we must qualify somewhat the saying that "the church exists to serve." This is true, but the church first of all exists as *the object of Jesus' love*. Because of this love, it will serve; this is the church's legitimate response. But Jesus wishes of his church, first of all, not service, but a healthy bride—whole, healthy, pure, loving, flourishing.

The church is constituted the church by the love of Christ, not by her service. She exists by grace through faith, not by works. She exists because Christ loved the church and gave himself for her, not because she "fulfills her mission in the world." But as she sees herself as the object of Jesus' love, in loving response she *will* carry out her mission in the world.

For the church is composed of persons, and the uniqueness of personhood comes from the image of God. So the church partakes of personality. This means she has worth simply for what she *is*, what she is constituted by the work of Christ, not primarily for what she *does*. Or, to use Martin Buber's terminology, she is a "Thou", not an It. God's relationship to the church—as well as to each specific member—is I–You, not I–It.

We see then that the concern of Scripture is that the church be built up as the body of Christ, and not merely fashioned as the instrument of Christ. This is the concern in fact of the whole of Ephesians 4. Spirit-inspired leaders are to prepare and equip the members for their ministry of edifying the body of Christ, until all attain to mature personhood.

In summary, we note three things about the leaders Paul mentions here:

1. They are based in spiritual gifts and are in this sense God-appointed.

2. Their primary function is the equipping of all the saints for their work of ministry.

3. Variety of ministries: the idea is not that of a professional class of "pastors" or "clergy," each of which is the sole leader in a local church.

Can we be more specific as to how these leaders should function in a local congregation? We have little biblical warrant for doing so. We do note however a relationship between the idea of *pastors and teachers*, or *pastor-teachers*, and what follows. Pastors and teachers have a supportive, equipping role in the church. What do they teach? What do they aim to produce in the local congregation? This is implied in the following verses.

First, they must teach, and produce, Christian unity (4:13). Second, they must help Christians grow to maturity, resulting in spiritually mature members (4:13-16). Third, they must teach sound doctrine as a defense against false doctrines (4:14). Fourth, they must produce a well-balanced relationship among the members through which each ministers to the other (4:16). (Interestingly John Wesley referred to this passage in describing the practical values that had accrued from his use of small groups, called "class meetings."[25])

---

[25] Howard A. Snyder, *The Radical Wesley*, rev. ed. (Franklin, Tenn.: Seedbed, 2014), 44.

Finally, these leaders must teach and produce Christian behavior (ethics) and holiness (4:17-24). This includes several things—relationships with one's neighbor (4:25-27), economic responsibility (4:28), conversation and speech (4:29) and, in general, Christ-like attitudes of love, tenderness, and a forgiving spirit (4:30-32).

These distinctions are somewhat artificial, for all these aspects overlap and are one. It is all a matter of growing up into Christ. Leadership and growth are an ecology, not a technology.

4:13-16 — The church is still conceived here as the body of Christ (4:12). This whole passage emphasizes the necessity of growing up into Christ, the head of the body. We have here also an interesting combination of the *personal* and *corporate* or shared aspects of the church in its growth to maturity. It is necessary that "we all" (i.e., each one) grow up into Christ—the particular, personal aspect. But this is in no isolated sense, for "the whole body, joined and knit together by every ligament with which it is equipped [i.e., each particular member], . . . promotes the body's growth in building itself up in love."

4:17-32 — These verses continue the same theme, with more specific application. (Note the parallel between 4:23-24 and Rom 12:1-2.)

What is significant here, from the standpoint of our theme, is that this whole passage focuses on the fact of the edification and growth-to-maturity of the church. There is no discussion here of the mission of the church in the world. The theme is the internal growth of the church. This is true, in large measure, of the rest of the epistle.

Is this not a rather introverted view of the church? The answer to this depends on one's presuppositions as to what is most important. We shall see that it is not an introverted view when properly understood.

Let us now look back over chapter four in light of Paul's basic theme. Ephesians shows us God's eternal plan for all creation through the church. How does chapter four contribute to this basic theme?

Essentially, Paul says three things in this chapter:

1. Lead a life worthy of God's plan for you.
2. Let the church grow up into the maturity of Christ.
3. God has provided for leadership in the church so that this really happens.

It is precisely, though not exclusively, in these ways that God will "gather up all things" in Christ; will manifest "the wisdom of God in its rich variety . . . to the rulers and authorities in the heavenly places; will glorify God through the church. How does this all fit together?

Paul is implying a key dynamic here. The church is to be the *demonstration* to the world (or to the "rulers and authorities") of God's wisdom, power, and glory. The church is to be the witness in the world of what God wishes to accomplish *and will accomplish* universally. The church is precisely in this sense the sign of the kingdom of God—the actual fulfillment in present history, on a limited basis, of God's eschatological design which is yet to be fulfilled, but which will certainly be fulfilled with Jesus' return to earth. Thus through the church the manifold wisdom of God may *now* be made known to the principalities and powers.

So it is vitally, crucially important what happens *within the church*. It is crucial that the church really demonstrate, in spacetime history, the reality of God's plan. This is the underlying truth of Paul's emphasis in this chapter.

There must be then, really, demonstration of *reconciliation* within the Christian community—reconciliation between God and persons and between and among the members of the Christian community. And the church, by its attitudes and actions, should bear witness also to the total reconciliation God brings, including the reconciliation between people and the whole creation.

Francis Schaeffer wrote very insightfully along this line in his book, *Pollution and the Death of Man: The Christian View of Ecology*. Schaeffer noted that in the Fall, "man"—that is humanity—

was divided from God, first; and then, ever since the Fall, man is separated from himself. These are the psychological divisions. I am convinced that this is the basic psychosis: that the individual [person] is separated from himself as a result of the Fall.

The next division is that man is divided from other men; these are the sociological divisions. And then man is divided from nature [i.e., creation], and nature is divided from nature. So there are these multiple divisions, and one day, when Christ comes back, there is going to be a complete healing of all of them, on the basis of the "blood of the Lamb."

But Christians who believe the Bible are not simply called to say "one day" there will be healing, but that by God's grace substantially, upon the basis of the work of Christ, substantial healing can be a reality here and now.[26]

Implicit here, of course, is the question of the church's

---

[26] Francis Schaeffer, *Pollution and the Death of Man: The Christian View of Ecology* (Wheaton, Ill.: Tyndale House, 1970), 67.

relationship to the world—the question of the church in society. We will leave this question to be discussed near the end of our comments, however, because of important material in chapters five and six.

Chapter 5

The Romance and Marriage of Christ's Body

In dramatic and rather surprising ways, Paul uses the image of marriage in this part of his letter. To grasp the full dimensions of this one would need to compare this chapter with the many other Scriptures where the marriage relationship is used as a metaphor (and more) for God's relationship to his people and to the world. Here however we focus specifically on Paul's teaching.

5:1 — *Therefore be imitators of God, as beloved children* —

Paul continues the ethical and moral applications and exhortations that go with the teachings previously laid out. His concern is that Christians be "imitators of God"—as God is revealed in Jesus Christ. Elsewhere Paul exhorts his converts to imitate *him*, as he faithfully follows the example of Christ.

5:2 — *And live [or walk] in love, as Christ loved us and gave himself up for us, a fragrant offering and sacrifice to God* —

Christians are to walk as Christ walked (1 Jn 2:6). This is essential to truly being the church. Jesus' life—and particularly his sacrificial death—provides the model for Christian living. We are to forgive as God forgives (4:32) and walk as Jesus walked (5:2).

The genuineness of our faith is measured not only by what we believe but also and especially by how we walk (cf. 2:10; 5:8, 15). This chapter may be considered an elaboration, to some extent, of the works that "God prepared beforehand, that we should walk in them" (2:10 RSV).

5:3-14 — Paul exhorts against immorality, impurity, undue levity (which we may take to be a fundamental lack of seriousness, not a blanket prohibition against all humor or against a proper sense of the ridiculous) and similar sins. The sincere Christian must walk in the light and "try to find out what is pleasing to the Lord" (5:10).

The parallel of this chapter with 1 John is striking, both in idea and terminology. This is all the more interesting since John and Paul usually express themselves in very different ways.

It is interesting also here that Paul uses the phrase "the kingdom of Christ and of God" (5:5). Some think that Paul didn't speak much in kingdom-of-God terms, but in fact he does in several places (Rom 14:17; 1 Cor 4:2, 6:9, 15:24, 15:50; Gal 5:21; Col 1:13, 4:11; 1 Thess 2:12; 2 Thess 1:5; 2 Tim 4:1, 4:18).

Note the following ways Paul speaks of the kingdom of God:

1. *Paul speaks frequently of "inheriting the kingdom"* (1 Cor 6:9, 15:50; Gal 5:2; Eph 5:5). This reminds us of Jesus' words in Matthew 25:34 ("Then the king will say to those at his right hand, 'Come, you that are blessed by my Father, inherit the kingdom prepared for you from the foundation of the world'") — and to the several references in the gospels to inheriting eternal life.

2. *Paul teaches that believers are now members of the kingdom* (Col 1:13, 4:11; 1 Thess 2:12), but that *the kingdom will come in fulness at Christ's second coming* (1 Cor 15:24, 15:50; 2 Tim 4:1, 4:18).

3. *The kingdom is characterized by righteousness, peace, joy* (Rom 14:17), *power* (1 Cor 4:2), *eternity* or everlastingness (1 Cor 15:50), and *glory* (1 Thess 2:12).

These teachings are strikingly similar to those in the gospels. Paul seems to have understood the kingdom in essentially the same way Jesus did. These ideas are in perfect harmony, for instance, with the parables of the kingdom.

It is particularly significant here that Paul, like Jesus, makes no direct identification between the church and the kingdom. The kingdom is an eschatological fact which is ever coming; we see its signs and know it will one day, in history, come in fulness. The church, the redeemed community, is the principal sign of the kingdom.

Since Paul says that God's plan is that *"through the church* the manifold wisdom of God might now be made known to the principalities and powers in the heavenly places" (3:10 RSV) it would seem that God is bringing in the kingdom of God primarily *through the church.* Yet this fact must be qualified in two ways: 1) History (both biblical and non-biblical) teaches us that God is at work also *outside* the church and at times in judgment *upon* the church; 2) The church is not capable on its own of bringing in the kingdom. Even with the mighty working of the Spirit within the church, the dominion of Satan working within the present world order is such that the kingdom of God can be brought in, in its fullness, only eschatologically—that is, by the return of Jesus Christ.

The church, then, is the principal sign of the kingdom. As earlier indicated, it is that community where God produces, in actual reality, a microcosm of his eternal and eschatological plan for humankind—that is, the fullness of the kingdom.[27]

5:6 — *because of these things the wrath of God comes on those who are disobedient* (cf. 2:2) —

This is the basis of judgment: God will judge people for their sinfulness. The wrath of God is coming. A biblical doctrine of the church must include the fact of divine wrath and judgment upon the "children of disobedience."

5:7 — *Therefore do not be associated with them* —

God's children are not to "associate" with the disobedient. There *is* a biblical doctrine of separation. But what does this mean? Verse 11 explains the sense in which Christians are not to associate with unbelievers: "Take no part in the unfruitful works of darkness, but instead expose them." The idea is not of association in terms of contact, but in terms of participation. God's children are not to be partakers with the children of disobedience in their sins and vices.

5:15-20 — Walking the Christian walk includes a proper (that is, fully biblical) perspective on all aspects of life. It includes the recognition of the value of time—something to be used wisely as part of our Christian stewardship, not to be squandered. We are to "understand what the will of the Lord is" (5:17); to "try to find out what is pleasing to the Lord" (5:10). There is much for us to learn—both what God expects of us personally and as a church, and more generally, what his cosmic plan really is.

Above all, our "intoxication" must come from the Holy Spirit,

---

[27] The reality and nature of the kingdom of God is elaborated in Howard A. Snyder, *Models of the Kingdom* (Nashville: Abingdon Press, 1991).

not from wine (5:18)—or, we might add, drugs or other substances. The Spirit's filling is the intoxication that elevates and liberates, not that which debauches and enslaves.

Paul emphasizes the need for joyful singing—"psalms and hymns and spiritual songs" (5:19). We don't need a detailed analysis of this verse; it is sufficient to note that these three words—psalms, hymns, and songs—mean about the same thing in Greek as in English. It is unnecessary to read anything more into the threefold usage.

Clearly the early Christians in fact used psalms, hymns, and other songs to express their worship. Music is necessary in the expression of the human spirit; it is undoubtedly in some way a part of the divine image in man and woman. A wide variety of kinds of music can and should be employed in praise to God because of the varieties of human tastes, personalities, and gifts, as well as cultural traditions. If this passage were to be reworded for our day, it would might say, "the hymns of the church, gospel songs, and new praise music."

The principle is that we should sing and make melody to the Lord with all our heart. This means especially that 1) the music should have the goal and actual function of praising or glorifying God, and 2) it should be a sincere expression, coming from the heart.

5:21 — *Be subject to one another out of reverence for Christ —*

This is the great governing principle for all that follows until 6:9. Here Paul applies Christian ethics—more specifically, what it means to be imitators of God in Christ (5:1-2)—to three key social relationships: husband–wife, parent–child, and master–slave.

5:22-33 — Paul elevates the marriage relationship to the highest possible level by comparing it to the relationship between Christ and the church. Immediately this alerts us to several things:

1. Marriage is holy. Within God's plan, especially as the union of two persons (man and woman) who already are part of the body of Christ, marriage is good, holy, beautiful, and beneficial.

2. Marriage is part of God's plan. It is more than a social convention, a cultural pattern that can be kept or discarded as a culture changes. There may be many different kinds of families, anthropologically speaking, but the basic relationships of marriage has divine sanction.

We may go further, in the light of homosexual tendencies in our age, and say that the relationship of *heterosexual* marriage has divine sanction or approval. Theologically and biblically, homosexual union—and especially "marriage"—is ungodly and contrary to creation, a fact so obvious, biblically speaking, that it should not need to be reiterated. The naturalness or propriety of homosexual unions can perhaps be supported on the basis of a blind evolutionary hypothesis, but not on the basis of a biblical view of human creation in God's image. I spell this out more fully in my small book, *Homosexuality and the Church*.[28]

3. Marriage is essentially a relationship of love. Once again, it is not *primarily* a social convenience or convention. Biblically, love is primary in marriage—but love biblically understood, not sentimentally or (exclusively) romantically defined.

4. The marriage relationship is not one of absolute

---

[28] Howard A. Snyder, *Homosexuality and the Church: Guidance for Community Conversation*, new ed. (Franklin, Tenn.: Seedbed Press, 2015).

equality. Rather, it is a relationship of what we might call equal symbiotic complementarity. This is clear from Paul's terminology here. There is equality of *worth*, of *responsibility*, of *value as persons* between husband and wife, though there may be difference of position or function. This often varies in different cultural contexts.

The husband has a preeminent position in regard to the wife as Christ does to the church. But this does not imply superiority and certainly not tyranny, since all is under the law of love. God has ordained this "functional arrangement" in which "the husband is the head of the wife," for in this way marriage is most harmonious. No marriage is more troubled than that in which both partners try to be the "head." In fact marriage should be an *equal partnership*, not a hierarchy. Harmonious partnership may involve or require diversification of function.

But note that "husband and wife" is not the same as "male and female." Gender is biologically determined, though gender *roles* in society are shaped by the cultural context. "Husband and wife" are cultural roles, not determined biologically. In some cultures and in some families, the assumed traditional role of husband may be filled by the woman, and the traditional role of wife may be filled by the man. A wide range of possibilities of mixing and sharing these roles is possible.

Paul's point here is that the love Jesus expresses for the church is the model for marriage. Husbands and wives are to love and care for each other in a Christ-like way as they work out the particular arrangement of roles and responsibilities that works best for them in their context.

In many traditional cultures, these roles are largely

predetermined by cultural patterns and expectations. In many societies today—certainly in the West, but increasingly worldwide—cultural expectations are much more flexible. So Christian couples must work out the best, most functional, and mutually nourishing relationships for them personally and in the context of their committed participation in the larger family of Christ, the church.

Although this passage seems to be more in harmony with a monogamous view of marriage—especially the quotation in verse 31—it would be forcing the text to say that the passage unequivocally teaches monogamy. If one wanted to argue for polygamy, they could point out that the relationship of Christ and the church is a union of one with many. But on the whole monogamy seems to be taken for granted in this passage.

5. The relationship between husband and wife is analogous to that between God and humans—and specifically here, between Christ and the church.

Since all life comes from God, it is natural that each kind of life is in ways similar to every other kind. Man and woman were equally created in the image of God. A part of that image is seen in the marriage relationship. In ways beyond our understanding, *the very division of human being into male and female is a reflection of the image of God* (Gen 1:27). There is something within the divine nature that requires or at least appropriately issues in this differentiation in humankind. Perhaps it is the plurality and intercommunication of the divine personality; perhaps it is something else. At heart, the universe is one; God is one. But this unity consistently shows itself in a diversity—the one divine Light refracted—and many times in a duality. The biblical Christian, in contrast to those of virtually every other religion or philosophy, recognizes that the obvious duality in the world does not indicate a basic essential duality in the universe, but is rather the way the one divine Unity chooses to self-express in creation.

In sum, this passage shows that the relationship between husband and wife is to be marked by the same love that throbs between Christ and the church.

This fact raises marital sexual union to the highest possible level of meaning and value. The fact that the marriage relationship is modeled after and reflects the divine-human relationship does *not* mean, as some have supposed, that marriage is spiritual to the exclusion or depreciation of the physical. This would imply a false dualism in human nature. Rather, the sexual union itself reflects and is analogous to the divine-human relationship. If sexual differentiation corresponds to or "echoes" something within the divine Nature, as we have argued, and if the human person is essentially a unity, then the very sexuality of man and woman, and the sexual union between husband and wife, also reflects something true about God's personhood.

This means we can legitimately say the reverse: the sexual union between husband and wife tells us something about the union of Jesus with his church. If it sounds almost obscene to see sex as analogous to Jesus' relationship with the church, this merely shows how debased our view of sex may be. Sex is, above all, *union of the most intimate and "fitting" nature on the basis of love*. It is physical and spiritual because the human person is physical and spiritual. God apparently is not physical. But the very physical marital relationship does not for this reason cease to reflect something true about the divine-human relationship since men and women, even in their physical bodies, bear the image of God.

To see how profound this fact of sex as a part of the image of God really is, it would be fruitful to make a detailed study of sex in the Bible, noting especially the many times sexual and/or marriage figures are used in describing the relationship between God and his people.

These, then, are some of the things we may learn in this passage concerning the marriage relationship. On the other side, what does this passage tell us about the church?

Perhaps the most suggestive aspect of this passage is the significance of the figures employed. We have here the blending of two different but related figures for the church: the figure of husband and wife, and the figure of head and body. The two are blended so that, in the case of the (literal) marriage relationship, the figure of head and body is used to explain the marriage relationship, just as the church is taken as a figure of marriage, and vice versa.

It is particularly significant that both these figures come from the realm of *human life*. Of all possible figures or analogies, these come nearest the very reality they symbolize. We may think of the church in relation to Christ in terms of vine and branches, of a building, or of potter and clay. But of all these, the two figures Paul employs here come the closest to the essence of the church.

These figures show us that, whatever else the church may be, its life in relation to Christ is living and *organic*, therefore *dynamic*; is based on *love* and *communication*; implies *interdependence* and at the same time the *preeminence* of the one (Christ, head, husband) in relation to the other (church, body, wife). The church's life is preeminently organic and dynamic, not organizational or institutional. It is a living, breathing thing.

This reinforces the thought, noted earlier, that the church as the body of Christ *is an end in itself*; it has supreme value precisely because it is the body and bride of Christ, the object of Christ's love. There is an essential difference between an institution and an organism at this point. An institution or organization is *a means to accomplish an end*; its value is determined by its utility in relation to accomplishing this end. In other words, it is a technique (cf. Ellul). But an organism—*life*—has value *in and of itself*. Biblically, life—and particularly human life—is of supreme worth because it is a reflection of the image of God. There is "that of God" in it constitutionally. The human person is essentially an end, not a means; he or she is a subject, not an object. How much more so the church!

All this is evident in what is said here about the relationship between Christ and the church. More specifically, this passage makes the following points about this relationship:

1. Jesus Christ is the head of the church. This affirmation is central to all that Paul says here. Jesus is head of the church for several reasons and in various senses. He is the Savior of the church (vs 23), her Lover (vs 25), her Sanctifier (vs 26). He "nourishes and tenderly cares for" the church (vs 29) and is, figuratively, the Husband of the church (vss 31-32).

The principal significance of this truth is, as we have noted, that the relationship between Christ and the church is a living one based on mutual love, and further, that the church depends on Christ for its existence—both for its creation and for its continuation. The church is the result of the action of Christ, both initially and throughout history.

2. Conversely, the church is the body of Christ. She is subject to Christ (vs 24), and is cleansed and nourished by him (vss 26, 19).

Thus she is, or should be, "holy and without blemish" (vs 27).
Finally, as the body of Christ the church is made up of a variety of
members (vs 30). She is no mere collection of separate persons. The
church takes on a real organic corporate existence, yet *is* composed
of particular believing persons.

Summary

Looking back now over chapter five, what more have we learned
about God's eternal plan through the church to unite all things in
Christ?

First, we note that the emphasis continues to be on *the integrity
of the Christian community as the body and bride of Christ.* It is
vital that the church actually manifest the character of Jesus Christ
(5:1-2, 25-27). This requires that the church exist in distinction
from, and therefore in judgment upon, the sinfulness of the world
(5:3-13). Implicit here is the fact that the church is an identifiable
community that exists in distinction from and in tension with
human society in general.

Secondly, there is a distinct attitude here of the rejection of
contemporary human society as non-Christian and godless. It is the
realm of "those who are disobedient" (5:6), of "the unfruitful works
of darkness" (5:11); evil days (5:16). This does not mean that
Christians should withdraw from the world or have no involvement
in human society, as Paul elsewhere makes clear. Rather the
principle is, "Take no part in the unfruitful works of darkness, but
instead expose them" (5:11). Exposure requires engagement with
society.

What does this say about God's eternal plan for the church? It
shows that the church must have no rosy optimism in regards to
society. She must not assume that society does not antagonize God

and the good, nor that society can easily—and/or gradually—be fully transformed into something good. God can and indeed does at times transform human society through the church in specific historical contexts. But this always occurs amid great struggle and resistance; and the transformation is never complete, because "the ruler of the power of the air" is "now at work among those who are disobedient" (2:2). Church history provides many examples of this.

This shows, then, that *God's eternal plan through the church will be accomplished through tension and conflict with human society, with the world.*

Every Christian believer, and the church itself, will live in tension with ungodly society. God's work of reconciliation takes place, for the time being, primarily *within the Christian community*, not within society in general. The person who becomes reconciled to God becomes part of the reconciled community, and thus *ceases* to be reconciled to the world. In becoming reconciled to God the new believer assumes a new life which at base is antagonistic to the world. Thus, for the time being, *the Christian community is the principal but not exclusive locus of God's reconciling work.*

Chapter 6

Powers Earthly and Heavenly

In chapter six Paul continues speaking to the Christian
community, exhorting and instructing them on the kind of life they
should live and the kind of relationships that should exist within the
body of Christ. Continuing the discussion of chapter five, Paul treats
here the relationship of parents to children (6:1-5) and masters and
slaves (6:5-9). With the "Finally" of 6:10, Paul brings the letter to a
conclusion with a remarkable and significant exhortation to the
Christian community in Ephesus.

6:1-4 — Paul is consistent with all biblical teaching in insisting
that children must obey their parents, as the Law itself commands.
This is a basic biblical principle which Christians, especially, must
affirm. The implication is not only that children must obey but,
conversely, that parents have a solemn responsibility to *teach* and
lovingly *require obedience* of their children as they are growing up.
But, crucially, all this is under the general principle already
enunciated in 5:21 — "Be subject to one another out of reverence to
Christ."

Note the structure here: after giving this general "mutual
submission" principle (5:21), Paul addresses both parties of three
basic relationships: marriage, family, and employment: wives (5:22)

and husbands (5:25), children (6:1) and fathers (6:4), slaves (6:5) and masters (6:9). In each case Paul mentions first the one who is subject to the other, but does not fail to speak also to the person who has authority over the other within the social-cultural context.

It should be emphasized that this requirement of obedience to parents is nowhere annulled in the Bible. It is valid for Christian and non-Christian alike—and, we may add, for the Christian child of non-Christian parents. A Christian child can justify disobedience to parents *only* when they require something contrary to obedience to Jesus Christ.

Paul balances the teaching here by laying responsibility also on the parents. They are to treat their children with love, patience, gentleness, and respect—all of which is implied in "do not provoke your children to anger." And they are to fulfill their duty of teaching and disciplining their children. The phrase "of the Lord" makes it clear that instruction in the truths of God (and therefore the Bible) is preeminent here. The Bible is supremely the book of instruction for raising children.

6:5-9 — *Slaves and masters* —

We learn from Paul's instructions here (as from other New Testament writings) that the early church had both slaves and masters among its members. This is significant and tells us something about the inclusive fellowship the early Christian community enjoyed.

The Lordship of Christ and the duty of obedience to him are used as the pattern for Christian behavior within the slave-master relationship.

Paul makes no direct attack on the institution of slavery. This actually hints at how revolutionary Paul's teaching really is here (especially in 6:9), and how the gospel in fact works to transform society and its structures through radical Christian community. In fact, Paul's teaching here embodies two powerful dynamics that cut to the very heart of slavery as an institution. The first is simply the fact that in the early church masters and slaves found themselves on equal footing within the community of faith. Slave or master, both entered the same way—through repentance and faith in Jesus Christ. Within the community, Jesus' love so permeated the atmosphere that all were brought to an equality of love.

This was the ideal and inherent reality, though early churches often embodied it perfectly. But reports of early church life indicate that this amazing equalizing of love was an observable reality within the local church.[29]

The second factor is the more explicit teaching Paul gives here: God is the master of both slave and human master and "with him there is no partiality" (6:9; cf. Rom 2:11). No partiality with God! This was revolutionary indeed. It meant that in the very basis of all existence—in the very person of God himself—all people are equal so far as social and economic position are concerned.

This teaching, stated or implied throughout the Bible, has powerfully worked in the Christian Church and in those societies where the church has been truly embodied. It has been a lamp to guide Christians in their social relations when they were obedient, and a thorn in their consciences when they were not. Christians

---

[29] Michael Green, *Evangelism in the Early Church* (Grand Rapids: Eerdmans, 1970); Alan Kreider, *The Patient Ferment of the Early Church: The Improbable Rise of Christianity in the Roman Empire* (Grand Rapids: Baker Academic, 2016).

could not (had they thought of it) have overthrown the social institution of slavery. But they could practically and powerfully undermine it within their own community. Like leaven, their influence spread out and the institution—which could never have been overthrown by force—withered away.

Here we have a practical illustration that shows how God's working *within* the Christian community affects society in general by creating a microcosm of the kingdom. Paul's concern is with the perfecting and growth of the Christian community, the body of Christ. This is his primary focus and *an end in itself.* But it has a big by-product— the eventual transformation of society.

This underscores what we noted earlier. The church is not to be understood as primarily a means to the end of transforming society. This would be to trample on the uniqueness and infinite worth to God of the Christian community. Besides, the amazing and profound fact is that the church most transforms society when it is itself growing and being perfected in the love of Christ (5:1-2). When the church is seen mainly as a means to transform society, really very little is accomplished. In that case, the very uniqueness of the church is denied and we enter the battle on the same terms as secular and godless forces. We assume the battle for right and justice can be won by *force*, by *technique*, by *doing*. It can't. Truly Christian transformation of society comes through *Christ-like* (hence sacrificial) *love*, through *community*; through *being*.

This is so important and so basic that the church is in mortal danger if it fails to learn it.

This is not an argument against moral reform in society or movements to bring social justice. Where such efforts and movements are possible, they can be powerful and effective. History provides many examples, such as the Abolitionist Movement in Britain and the United States in the 1800s. These movements would never have happened, however, if it hadn't been for the "patient ferment" (Alan Kreider's phrase) of Christian social witness over centuries.

What we have said about slavery could be said also about marriage and the treatment of children, the two subjects Paul already dealt with. Demonstrating truly Christian virtues and truths within the Christian community in these areas becomes leaven transforming society in the areas of family and labor relations.

6:10-12 — Here begins Paul's exhortation to "put on the whole armor of God." But what most impresses us in these first verses is the description of the enemy: "For our struggle is not against enemies of blood and flesh, but against the rulers, against the authorities, against the cosmic powers of this present darkness, against the spiritual forces of evil in the heavenly places."

Here once again we have the church set in cosmic perspective. Our struggle is not primarily with "flesh and blood" but with the "principalities and powers."

We have already discussed the meaning of these cosmic references at some length (see discussion of 3:9-10). Here we see who and what are the true enemies of the church. It is the kingdom of Satan, which includes "the rulers, . . . the authorities, . . . the cosmic powers of this present darkness, . . . the spiritual forces of evil in the heavenly places." As we have already shown, this includes all earthly forces and powers structures that are in the service of evil.

How then does the church engage in battle against these forces?

This is the subject of the remaining part of this section on the armor of God.

6:13-20 — Many devotional studies have been made of this passage. Our purpose here however is to understand this passage, not primarily in its devotional value to lone Christians, but for what it tells us of the church's battle with evil and its fulfilling of the cosmic plan of God. This in fact is Paul's main intent.

6:13 — *Therefore take up the whole armor of God, so that you may be able to withstand on that evil day, and having done everything, to stand firm.* The church is engaged in a spiritual battle, and its weapons are spiritual—"the whole armor of God." *It is with these weapons, and these weapons alone, that the church can and must confront the principalities and powers, the power structures, visible and invisible.*

What are the weapons and defenses of the church? What a strange list we have here, when compared to the weapons that are judged effective and necessary by worldly standards! These are the legitimate weapons of the church: truth, righteousness, the gospel of peace, faith, salvation, the Word of God, prayer and supplication, and the bold proclamation of the mystery of the gospel. A brief study of each of these weapons reveals their uniqueness and power.

Truth — The first weapon of the church is truth. In military and political warfare it is propaganda. Propaganda in warfare is truth as a tool to be twisted according to the end desired; it is not sacred in itself. But with the church it must not be so. There must be strict adherence to truth in every sense; there must be no compromising of the truth, for God is the God of truth. Jesus Christ is the truth (Jn

14:6). The church must not be "conformed to this world" (Rom 12:2) but must be "conformed to the image" of Jesus Christ (Rom 8:29) and to the true nature of her mission and being in this matter of truth. Although we live in the world, "we do not wage war according to human standards; for the weapons of our warfare are not merely human, but they have divine power to destroy strongholds" (2 Cor 10:3-4).

Righteousness — In human warfare, righteousness is a victim in almost every sense. Though righteous people have been involved in war and people have often considered their cause righteous, it remains true that there is no such thing as "a righteous war" (although just war theory makes allowance for necessary force to resist evil in very specific circumstances).

The Christian community must be clothed in righteousness. Its very character thus becomes a weapon, a defense (breastplate) against "the spiritual forces of evil." War is the enemy of righteousness, but in the spiritual warfare of the church righteousness and justice must be a primary weapon.

The Gospel of Peace — "As shoes for your feet put on whatever will make you ready to proclaim the gospel of peace" (6:15), or "the preparedness which comes from the gospel whose message is peace" (*EGT*). Genuinely possessing or experiencing the gospel is itself a weapon, a preparation—obviously, an essential one — for the Christian warfare. And specifically, this is the gospel of peace! Peace with God, of course; but in the most abundant sense the gospel of Christ is the Gospel of peace, *shalom*. The gospel is the very antithesis of all that brings strife and violence and war in human affairs. It is supremely and always the gospel of peace.

Faith — Salvation is by faith, and without faith it is impossible to please God. This faith is the supreme defense against "all the flaming arrows of the evil one." So John: "This is the victory that conquers the world, our faith" (1 Jn 5:4).

Secular or jihadist warfare as well as secular psychology recognize the defensive value of *faith*. Faith is functional. In military warfare, it is essential that the combatants have full faith in their cause—whether it be nationalism, Nazism, Communism, "the American Way of Life," religious radicalism, or whatever. In military warfare, the fact of faith *in itself* is the thing; the basis of this faith is secondary. In human warfare, faith becomes a technique, in effect, a weapon. Whether there is a valid basis for faith or not is unimportant, so long as the participants *believe* in their cause.

This "believism" pervades much of contemporary society (not just Protestantism). The important thing is to *believe*; it matters little *what* you believe.

Against such a neutered concept of faith, biblical Christianity rightly protests—whether such faith is encountered in secular society, popular pulpit Christianity, or theology. *Of course* faith is functional. But when we are dealing with one's relationship to God and warfare with evil, the all-important question is the *object* of that faith. In the church's battle with "the spiritual forces of evil in the heavenly places," only a valid and living faith in the person of Jesus Christ will suffice.

The "shield of faith" (6:16) which is efficacious results from the presence of Jesus Christ the Spirit in the life of the believer.

Salvation — "The helmet of salvation" (6:17) implies another defensive weapon. But we must not press the symbolism too far. In a sense the "shield of faith" and the "helmet of salvation" say the same thing. As Christians we need the complete work of salvation in our shared lives.

The Word of God — The Word of God is here called "the sword of the Spirit" (6:17; cf. Heb 4:12; Rev 1:16, 19:15). It seems obvious here, as elsewhere in the Scriptures, that the "word of God" in this passage means more than the Bible. It is a dynamic reality including, preeminently, Jesus Christ as the living Word.

The Word of God is the church's primary offensive weapon. While this certainly includes the Bible, it means more than the Scriptures. It means the living action of Christ the Word, Christ the Spirit, in the life of the church. There is never conflict between Jesus Christ the living Word and the Bible as the written Word. Certainly the Scriptures are themselves a primary weapon of the church.

Paul says nothing about how to use this weapon. It is merely to be "taken" and used. How does one in fact use the Word of God?

First of all, we must obey it. Thus we discover that the Word to be sharp and active (Heb 4:12) *in our own lives*. The Word of God is an effective weapon, in the first instance, because of what it does in the life of each Christian believer and in the shared life of Christian community.

Does this mean that, in the Christian warfare, the most important thing is what God through his Word accomplishes in the Christian community? Yes—precisely! This fits in with all we have been seeing in Ephesians about the nature of the church. The most crucial thing in the church's spiritual warfare with the principalities and powers is not what she *does*, but who she *is*.[30]

---

[30] Kreider emphasizes this point in *The Patient Ferment of the Early Church*.

So, church, "Take the Word of God"! Let Christ the Word work within you. Be obedient to the Word, and it will transform your life, transform the very church into a weapon for righteousness in the battle for truth.

Prayer and Supplication — "Pray in the Spirit at all times in every prayer and supplication" (6:18). Paul recommends prayer specifically for himself and "for all the saints."

Prayer is crucial because it is the church's main means of contact with God; it is what unites the body of Christ with the Head. It is the necessary communication between God and the church through which the *koinonia* of the Holy Spirit is maintained.

And in making prayer "for all the saints"—that is, for all believers—the church upbuilds itself in love. The first concern of each believer is, properly, the welfare of his or her brothers and sisters in Christ. As God acts in each believer the body is built up, and all benefit. And as the body grows, as its fellowship is increasingly genuine and godly, the church also has its intended influence and ministry in the world.

So prayer (including "supplication" and intercession) is a most important weapon. By it the church is strengthened and built up. Paul does not here specifically mention prayer for those outside the church, for the world, which of course is always appropriate. Rather he speaks here of that kind of prayer through which the church itself is edified in Christ. On this prayer depends the survival of the church, for it is only by maintaining its vital, "vertical" contact with Jesus Christ the Spirit that the church is kept from becoming a purely human or this-worldly social entity.

The Bold Proclamation of the Gospel — Paul asks for prayer that he may be enabled "boldly" to proclaim "the mystery of the gospel"

(6:19-20). Paul does not specifically list this as one of the weapons that make up the "whole armor of God." Yet we sense Paul's passion for gospel proclamation, and we realize it's an important responsibility of the church to proclaim the gospel boldly. As we have seen throughout this study, what the church *is*, as a redeemed community, is of primary importance. It is on the basis of its authentic *being* that the Christian community is able to proclaim, convincingly and with integrity, the truth of the gospel. If the church's community in Jesus Christ is not genuine, its proclamation will be hollow.

6:21-22 — Paul's concern that the Ephesian Christian community have a personal update about himself prompts him to send Tychicus as his messenger so he may "tell you everything" and thus "encourage your hearts." Paul always had around him one or more young men—brothers, assistants, apprentices—as well as several key women. Colleagues like Tychicus helped him and he trained them to carry on his ministry. This was his pattern, as suggested by 2 Timothy 2:2 and several other passages. As with Jesus, a vital part of Paul's ministry was such one-to-one contact by which he built intensively into a network of key lives.

6:23-24 — Peace, love, faith, and grace. With these, some of the greatest and most uniquely characteristic words and realities of the Christian faith, Paul closes his letter.

Conclusion

God's Power in Today's Church

We can now review what we have learned in this letter about God's cosmic plan through the church and draw together those things which are most crucial for our day. We can outline the principal teachings of the Holy Spirit in Ephesians as follows:

1. **God has an eternal and cosmic plan which is to be accomplished in strategic part through the church.** It is of course the purpose of all biblical revelation to give us this plan, so what we learn in Ephesians must be taken in context with the whole Bible. Yet Ephesians, in a remarkably suggestive and concentrated way, gives us the essential points, the key elements of this plan.

2. **This plan centers in the incarnation, life, death, resurrection, and ongoing work of Jesus Christ.** Jesus is the central figure of the book and of God's plan. Without Jesus Christ—without his life, death, and resurrection in space, time, and history—there would be no plan. What Paul has written here would be nonsense.

3. **The purpose and goal of God's plan can be summed up in two words: reconciliation, redemption.** It is to redeem people from sin, yes—and in fact to reconcile all things to God through Christ, as we have seen. Taken in light of the full biblical picture of salvation, this redeeming reconciliation means healing, restoration, and the full flourishing of creation (*shalom*) as the kingdom of God comes in fullness.

We may describe four dimensions of this salvation, this reconciliation, as Paul pictures it in Ephesians. To be biblical, we must not deny to neglect any of these.

a. *God's plan is particular and personal.* That is, it involves the salvation of specific persons, and their reconciliation to God. It should be self-evident that this is the primary or central dimension of salvation, given the fact that God is person and humans bear his image. The nature of persons as moral and spiritual beings places their relationship to God on a higher plane than God's relationship to the rest of creation, though clearly this is not an either/or.[31] Personal salvation is not the *limit* or *circumference* of God's plan, but it is its center. Without personal salvation the other aspects would make no sense. Personal redemption through the blood of Jesus Christ is the first dimension.

b. *God's plan is corporate—through the church.* We see throughout Ephesians how God's plan involves the church; how it is specifically *through the church* (3:10) that God is accomplishing his plan. The point is that God does not save the isolated "individual." Rather, his personal salvation places each believer within a body— the church, the body of Christ. Believers personally become members of the body from which they draw strength and to which they contribute strength. So the body "builds itself up in love" (4:16), with the fullness of Jesus Christ the Head as the goal of this growth-to-maturity.

So God is not only saving persons; he is saving the church as the community of reconciled persons, *as the model of the cosmic*

---

[31] See Francis Schaeffer's excellent exposition of this point in *The God Who Is There*, 94ff.

reconciliation God has ultimately planned and, to a large degree, as the very *agent* of that reconciliation.

c. *God's plan is social—it involves the social and cultural relationships of believers.* Paul shows in Ephesians how the reconciliation God brings must extend to all our social relationships. Ephesians specifically deals with four relationships: Jew–Gentile, husband–wife, parent–child, and master–slave. Yet clearly God's plan is much broader than this, for it is "the reconciliation of all things," both heavenly and earthly, visible and invisible.

The accent on doing the *works* God prepared beforehand (2:10) also comes in here. The church lives and acts to *demonstrate* reconciliation before and within society and its power structures (3:10), including politics and economics. This is a form of judgment, yet it also has a reconciling, redeeming effect—like leaven—throughout society. Thus the church is the sign of the kingdom which *is* coming, and *will come* in fullness with the return of Christ. All God's promises will be fulfilled.

d. *God's plan is cosmic.* Its final goal is the reconciliation of all things, things in heaven and things on earth, visible and invisible. We have noted this prominent and recurrent cosmic aspect throughout Ephesians. If we miss this dimension of God's plan, we will have a dwarfed view of the church, of personal salvation, of God's will for people, and thus of mission. The opposite danger, of course, is making cosmic redemption so primary that personal redemption is eclipsed.

4. The church, essentially, is the community of God's people. This is the true nature of the church as body of Christ. Biblically the church is not an organization, a hierarchical structure, an institution, nor merely a means toward accomplishing an end. Biblically understood, it is a community empowered, indwelt, and directed by the living Spirit of Jesus Christ.

Several things need to be said about the nature of this community:

a. *The church is essentially a spiritual reality.* Its true nature is spiritual—not "spiritual" in the sense of being radically distinct from "earthly" or "physical," but spiritual in the sense that its essential nature transcends the limits of space and time. It is now "in the heavenlies" in the sense in which Paul uses that phrase in Ephesians.

This means that whatever one perceives sensually as "church"—buildings, organizations, institutions, and so forth—is not truly the church. Whether such things are in fact a betrayal of the true nature of the church will have to be decided on the basis of a clear understanding of the biblical nature of the church and God's plan through the church, and on an analysis of how these things (buildings, organizations, creeds, and so forth) actually function either to serve and extend the church's life and witness or to subvert or compromise it.

b. *The church is an end in itself, not merely a means toward an end.* True, it is "through the church" that God is accomplishing his eternal plan, so in an important sense the church does serve instrumentally. But this sense is the same as is always true when God works through human beings: He works in a way that does not violate the worth and value of human personality but rather enhances and ennobles it.

It is thus with the church, as we have noted in our comments on

Ephesians 5:22-33. The church is a living organism; it has been made alive by Christ (2:1ff). So it is of worth to God for what it *is*, quite apart from what it *does*. In fact, as we have also seen, in large measure it accomplishes God's plan by *being* what God intends. It is this being alone that provides the basis for doing the works which God prepared beforehand. So we can legitimately say that the church essentially is an end, not a means; that the church is essentially a living organism, not an organization. This is another way of saying in fact that our warfare is spiritual, not carnal.

This is a way of saying also that the church is a community of persons relationally connected with the Triune God, three Persons in one intercommunion. Each person is important; every relationship is important; and what each person does within and as an outward expression of this relationship is important.

c. *There is a divinely-revealed plan for leadership within the church.* This is outlined, as we have seen, in Ephesians 4:7-16. God promises here that through the operation of the Holy Spirit he will give his church the leaders that are truly necessary so that the body may function as body.

Specifically, God gives to the church apostles, prophets, evangelists, pastors and teachers. This work of the Spirit is a gift of *persons*, not *offices*. No hierarchical organizational structure is implied or intended here. Yet the necessity of leadership is recognized and provided for. Each of these leaders is important and necessary in the church, and their function is "to equip the saints for the work of ministry, for building up the body of Christ, until all of us come to the unity of the faith and of the knowledge of the Son of God, to maturity, to the measure of the full stature of Christ" (4:12-13). In the notes we have indicated more fully the function of each of these leaders.

5. How God's plan through the church is accomplished.

Ephesians does not tell us in detail or in a programmatic way how God works out his plan through the church. But it does give very basic and crucial information showing what the church ought to *be* and ought to be *doing* in order that this plan may be fulfilled. These aspects can be outlined as follows:

a. *God's plan through the church begins with personal conversion.* This is the indispensable first step Paul—and all the New Testament—consistently stress. It is being "made alive," "saved by faith," "born again." This is the beginning of personal spiritual life and thus also the beginning of the church. For the church to have life, there must be birth. (We recognize of course that God's preceding or "prevenient" grace is already at work drawing people to Jesus and new life in him well before a person comes to conscious personal saving faith.)

b. *God's plan through the church involves the filling of the Holy Spirit and the Spirit's indwelling presence* as a fact in each disciple's life and in the Christian community. The Spirit fills each believer and empowers, energizes, and unites the body in love.

c. *God's plan through the church requires that the church be a living demonstration of the community and reconciliation that God has provided for and is accomplishing through Jesus Christ.* As we have emphasized throughout the notes, the church is first of all to *be* something, rather than to *do* something. It is called to be a microcosm of God's reconciliation, a demonstration to the world (to the "rulers and authorities," or "principalities and powers") of the reality of human community based in Jesus Christ.

These first three aspects, of course, relate almost exclusively to the interior life of the church rather than to Christian life in the world. Any biblically valid understanding of God's plan must begin with proper emphasis on personal conversion and life together in Christian community.

But how do we move beyond this to show how Christians are (how the church is) to be agents of reconciliation in the world? How do we biblically move from the fact of *being* to the fact of *doing*? Ephesians gives us several suggestive and significant clues. We need to relate these clues, however, to what God reveals elsewhere in Scripture.

Second Corinthians 5 is especially helpful here, because it makes the link between the fact that God has reconciled us to himself and that God's plan is the reconciliation of all things. Here we learn that God "reconciled us to himself through Christ, and *has given us the ministry of reconciliation*" (2 Cor 5:18). Crucially, a ministry of reconciliation has been entrusted to the church.

This ties in with what we have seen regarding Ephesians 2:10 and 3:10. Theologically, these two verses can legitimately be linked together as follows: "We are what he has made ["his workmanship," RSV], created in Christ Jesus for good works, which God prepared beforehand, to be our way of life, that through the church the wisdom of God in its rich variety might now be made known to the rulers and authorities in the heavenly places."

So the church is called not only to *be* (Eph 2:8-9), but also to *do* (2:10). In the true, living body of Christ, in fact, *being* and *doing* are of course inseparable. It is the nature of all the living creatures God has made—and supremely of the church — to both *be* and *do*; that is, to act consistently with its authentic nature.

But when we speak of Christians as agents of reconciliation, we have also to recognize such passages as Eph 5:3-18. Here we learn that there is a fundamental tension between the church (and so each believer) and the world. So, as Christ prayed, Christians must be *in* the world but *kept from* the world in the sense of being overcome by it. The church takes seriously its separateness from the world even as it seeks to work for reconciliation in the world.

With these distinctions in mind, we can now continue our summary of God's plan through the church.

d. *God's plan through the church requires, fourthly, that the church be in the world as an agent of reconciliation.* As agent of reconciliation, it is a demonstration to the principalities and powers of the wisdom, power, and glory of God.

1) The church must exist as a distinct community in the world, as a light that exposes evil. This distinctness is necessary for real reconciliation. It must shine as a light that is not overcome by the darkness of godless society.

2) The church's ministry of reconciliation begins with judgment. The motto is, "Take no part in the unfruitful works of darkness, but instead expose them" (5:11). Here the church follows the model of her Lord—Jesus Christ, the great reconciler, who became judgment on his world. Jesus' attitude toward the world of his day tells us much about how reconciliation begins. A faithful church is itself judgement,

without being judgmental in attitude.

3) The church as the redeemed community, as a model of the future reconciliation of all things, is a *witness* to God's basic intention in the world: reconciliation, redemption, healing, restoration. It shows what the nature of God's plan is, being thus a witness to the kingdom of God.

4) The church actually becomes the locus of reconciliation in that through the church persons actually do become reconciled to God.

a) This means the church must actually be involved in the *proclamation* of the gospel message, as implied in 3:8, 13 and 6:19. God gives those to the church whose function it is to "boldly proclaim the mystery of the gospel."

b) This also means welcoming and integrating into the body of Christ those who respond to the message so that they actually do become reconciled to God and other believers and the body "builds itself up in love."

e. *God's plan through the church suggests that every Christian is in the world as a minister of reconciliation.* This means each Christian actually doing the good works which God has prepared beforehand (2:10).

While Paul does not extensively elaborate this theme, clearly something very important is implied here. We are faced here with the fact of God's plan as it relates to the life and work of each particular believer—in other words, the fact of *vocation*. God calls each believer to some "work of ministry" within the body of Christ. But his will also extends to each Christian's total being and doing in the world. Here also the Christian disciple is a minister of reconciliation, called to walk in the works God has prepared from the foundation of the world. What an overwhelming, cosmic concept of personal vocation!

Since Paul does not spell out for us here just what such vocation might involve in the world, we cannot detail the various ministries of reconciliation that may be possible. But since it is God's plan to reconcile to himself all things in Christ—things visible and invisible, heavenly and earthly—and accomplish this through the church—we are on firm ground in saying that *wherever* a Christian is working for reconciliation in the world, working to heal the brokenness of the world and heal the breaches opened by the fall, there God is at work and there is a sign of the kingdom of God.

The kingdom of God is all about *radical social reconstruction*, that all may be in harmony with God's will and good purposes. This Jesus began, continues, and will bring to completion. This is the work of Jesus' followers, the body of Christ.

As for the specifics of such work of ministry in the world, we have the model of Jesus Christ. This model is relevant here in at least three ways:

1) *The example and model of Christ's life*—what Jesus actually did, how he actually lived in the world. Jesus' life and actions provide hints and clues as to possible legitimate ministries of reconciliation in the world.

2) *The model of the Sermon on the Mount.* Jesus' teachings here cannot be dismissed as having no or only generalized relevance or application for Christians today. Again, there are hints and suggestions here relating to

Christian vocation in the world, kinds of ministries of reconciliation.

3) *The model of the parables of the kingdom.* These are very suggestive concerning the relationship of the church and each believer to society, and of the role and impact of the Christian influence—*through the lived lives of Christians*—in society. Lives and ministries in harmony with these parables are true ministries of reconciliation. Perhaps the most suggestive of these parables is that of leaven.

The key here is for every believer to find the basis of his or her life, involvement, and integration in the life of the Christian community—and on that basis, to find God's will for his or her life *in the world*. God has a plan for each person's journey that should involve each Christian in some work with eternal reconciling significance.

At all the points of alienation in the world, Christians should be working as ministers of reconciliation. They should be working in the world for reconciliation between persons, between people and society, and between people and nature. All these relationships were harmonious at creation but disrupted at the Fall. Christians will never heal them *completely*; this depends on a cosmic act of God through the return of Christ. But through the Spirit they may heal them partially and substantially in specific places, as a witness to God's will and plan and as signs of the coming kingdom.

This is God's plan through the church.

About the Author

Howard A. Snyder currently serves as International Representative of the Manchester Wesley Research Centre in England. He has taught at Tyndale Seminary in Toronto (2007 2012), Asbury Theological Seminary (1996 2006), United Theological Seminary in Dayton, Ohio (1988 1996), and in Chicago and São Paulo, Brazil. His two dozen books include *The Problem of Wineskins*, *The Community of the King*, *Salvation Means Creation Healed* (with Joel Scandrett), and most recently *Jesus and Pocahontas: Gospel, Mission, and National Myth* (2015).

INDEX

www.ingramcontent.com/pod-product-compliance
Lightning Source LLC
Chambersburg PA
CBHW072144090426
42739CB00013B/3273